Aging Mastery® Playbook by James Firman and Susan Stiles.

Published by National Council on Aging,

251 18th Street, Suite 500, Arlington, VA 22202.

www.ncoa.org

© 2018 National Council on Aging

Cover by Matthew Baek.

ISBN: 978-0-692-99613-3

Aging Mastery®
PLAYBOOK

James Firman, EdD
Susan Stiles, PhD

National Council on Aging
Arlington, Virginia
2018

Table of Contents

INTRODUCTION 3

Section I: Aging Mastery® and the Gift of Time

1.1 THE AGING MASTERY® JOURNEY 6

1.2 A PLAYBOOK FOR YOU 16

Section II: The Six Dimensions of Aging Well

2.1 GRATITUDE AND MINDFULNESS 24

2.2 HEALTH AND WELL-BEING 36

2.3 FINANCES AND FUTURE PLANNING 66

2.4 CONNECTIONS AND COMMUNITY 90

2.5 CREATIVITY AND LEARNING 108

2.6 LEGACY AND PURPOSE 123

Section III: Activities

3.1 GETTING STARTED 138

3.2 ACTIVITIES FOR EACH DIMENSION OF
AGING WELL 146

3.3 AGING MASTERY® GUIDEPOSTS 162

ENDNOTES 165

INTRODUCTION

Greetings and welcome to Aging Mastery®!

The Aging Mastery® Playbook is designed to be a springboard to help you focus on positive behaviors that will enable you to address the new realities of aging. You'll be prompted to take small steps that will make your life better and motivate you to help others. Along the way, this book will encourage you to AMPlify your thinking about growing older and also AMPlify your behavior.

We will ask you to think closely about what growing older means to you and to challenge your preconceptions. Our hope is that we can inspire you to overcome the mental hurdles that might prevent you from changing the things that are in your power to change, and to make positive changes in your life

Where to start? As the king in *Alice in Wonderland* said, "Begin at the beginning." We encourage you to read **Section I** first. This section will give you a good foundation in the basics of Aging Mastery®, put you in the mindset of building your Aging Mastery® core team, and get you started on your Aging Mastery® journey. **Section II** addresses the six dimensions of aging. It can be read in any order that you like and we encourage you to both read and re-read this section. **Section III** includes suggested activities that will help you as you incorporate the AMP Guideposts into your daily routines.

Our promise to you:

1. We will share with you what we've learned about aging well across six dimensions.

2. We will offer suggestions for small behavior changes that we know can make a big difference.

3. We will encourage you to chart your own path for aging well. After all, it's **your** life!

Your promise to us:

1. You will commit to making one positive behavior change in each of the six dimensions of aging.

Sound like a deal? Let's learn about Aging Mastery®.

AGING MASTERY® AND THE GIFT OF TIME

1.1 THE AGING MASTERY® JOURNEY

"Hmmm—I thought the flower would bloom by itself."

A flower knows its purpose in life: It must bloom. For people, understanding our purposes in life and making those a reality will likely be lifelong pursuits. Along the way, we will set many goals. Think of these as single blooms that, together, form a large, flowering plant. Each phase of life brings with it specific goals and pursuits. Our "golden years" should be no different. We should be constantly growing, constantly blooming—with intention and with the responsibility to be true to our purpose. And, it is up to us to define that purpose.

Emily Dickinson wrote a poem that illustrates this idea well. The poem also points to some central themes we would like you to keep in mind as you read this book and as you go about your daily activities.

We encourage you to read the poem[1] a couple of times:

> Bloom—is Result—to meet a Flower
> And casually glance
> Would scarcely cause one to suspect
> The minor Circumstance
>
> Assisting in the Bright Affair
> So intricately done
> Then offered as a Butterfly
> To the Meridian—
>
> To pack the Bud—oppose the Worm—
> Obtain its right of Dew—
> Adjust the Heat—elude the Wind—
> Escape the prowling Bee
>
> Great Nature not to disappoint
> Awaiting Her that Day—
> To be a Flower, is profound
> Responsibility—

It's a beautiful poem, isn't it? And powerful, too. Let's consider it carefully.

What does it take for a flower to bloom? In short, a lot: It takes work, energy, persistence, intentionality, flexibility, creativity, and even some craft to "oppose the worm" and many other obstacles, and rise out of the earth. There's nothing coincidental about it. Full bloom is the "Result" of something, not just something that happens automatically to the flower. All the hard work, the care, and the thought may not be apparent to everyone else, though. Others "casually glancing" might not see the effort and skill that brings the bloom to the light of day.

But that hardly matters. The flower answers to Nature and will not disappoint her. It fulfills its responsibility by blooming. And—this is key—it takes this responsibility "profoundly" seriously.

AMPlify Your Thinking

Take some time to reflect on your life and your life's goals—what you have done, what you are currently doing, and where you would like to go from here.

- What have you had to do to bloom (to reach your goals)?
- What obstacles have you overcome?
- What ingenuity have you used?
- What is your responsibility now so you can continue to bloom?
- Are you prepared to challenge yourself with new goals?

THE GIFT OF TIME

The gift of time is real. As a result of advances in medicine and technology, many of us will live a lot longer than our parents or grandparents. Longevity is a word that we hear quite a bit in the context of these scientific advances. There are longevity institutes and innovation centers springing up across the country and around the world. Often, additional words such as "anti-aging," "aging in place," and "aging well" are used in conjunction with the word "longevity". One thing is for certain: The pursuit of the fountain of youth is alive and well!

But focus groups conducted by the National Council on Aging (NCOA) show that most people do not see value in longevity just for the sake of living longer. They value *quality of life* over quantity of life.

The gift of time is real. Life expectancy has increased dramatically over the past 50 years, which is great news. Importantly, not only are we living longer, but we are also in overall better health during our retirement years than previous generations.

> *"Time is the coin of your life. It is the only coin you have, and only you can determine how it will be spent."*
>
> — *Carl Sandburg*

In 1950, the average American who was age 65 could expect to live another 14 years in retirement with about half of that time in good health. Today, once people reach age 65 they can expect to live, on average, another 19 years (men a bit less, women a bit longer) with roughly two-thirds of that time in good health.[2] As a result, we can expect to have the greatest amount of free, unscripted time in history.

Here's another amazing fact: Experts estimate[3] that more than half of those born in industrialized nations since the year 2000 will live into the triple digits. Wow.

Yes, aging has changed remarkably since the last generation entered retirement, and it continues to change. However, societal expectations have not kept up with these changes. (The societal infrastructure to support increased longevity is lacking, too, but that is a topic for another book!) For example, people aged 65–74 spend the majority of their time[4] either sleeping (nine hours per day) or engaging in leisure activities (about eight hours daily). This includes an average of 4.5 hours per day watching TV. Very little time (about one hour per day) is spent doing things that proactively contribute to their own well-being and that of others. We have the greatest amount of free time in history. How are we spending that time? Can we, and should we, be doing more with our time?

The gift of time is real. For some of us, that statement may not ring true. It may sound far-fetched, or even cruel, especially if we lost a loved one to accident or illness before they lived out a long life. And yet, if we compare our generation to previous generations, the data is compelling. The probability of living longer and in better health is strong. Now, let's consider how you can make the most of it and continue to bloom.

AGING MASTERY®

Making the most of your gift of time is where Aging Mastery® comes into the picture.

Aging Mastery® celebrates the gift of longer lives. It aims to change societal expectations about the roles and responsibilities of older adults. It also seeks to create fun and easy-to-follow pathways for getting more out of life.

For most of us, it is not enough to be told that we need to exercise daily or save more. We need specific, engaging opportunities that motivate and support us to take positive action. The Aging Mastery® approach looks to help individuals create **sustained changes in daily habits and behaviors**. The advantage of changing habits is that once behaviors become automatic, we no longer have to use as much energy or willpower to maintain healthy decisions. Gretchen Rubin calls habit "the invisible architecture of everyday life" and notes that approximately 40% of what we do every day, we do in pretty much the same way and in the same context.[5] So, if we can change a range of important habits as we age, we're much more likely to be happier, healthier, and more productive.

Modest lifestyle changes can and do produce long-lasting results. **We believe that if older adults spend just a bit more time each day on positive behavior change**, it will lead to higher levels of **physical** and **emotional well-being**, improved **financial security**, increased **civic engagement**, and stronger **social connectedness**.

We also need to view our lives as a totality. We know that nothing happens in isolation. A health issue can impact our pocketbook which might then limit our social activities, living

situation, family relationships, and more. Aging Mastery®
encourages people to look at their actions via a wide array of
lenses that include mindfulness, nutrition and fitness, sleeping
patterns, relationships, economic health, civic engagement,
advance care planning, creativity, and other vital topics.

Aging Mastery® is an approach to living, not a prescription
for living. This distinction is very important. Underlying Aging
Mastery® are three core elements: autonomy, mastery, and
purpose. These principles were spelled out by Daniel Pink[6], an
author who writes on business, work, and behavior, to explain
how to motivate employees, but we think they work very well
for older adults, too. The key ideas are that you decide what
you will do (autonomy); if you are going to do something, you
want to see progress (mastery); and whatever you do should be
meaningful (purpose).

Let's look at each of these through the lens of Aging Mastery®.

Autonomy: You are in charge of your life and you decide
how you will spend your time. Our goal is to provide you with
information to help you make the choices that are right for you.
To help you decide, we will suggest a few options, because we
know that when people have too many options, they usually
don't choose any of them. However, if you want to substitute
another similar action, go right ahead. Also, remember that
doing nothing is a choice as well.

Mastery: When people decide to do something, they want to
know that they are progressing. This book is a starting point for
you to begin to make and measure progress. Aging Mastery® is
a marathon, not a sprint. The key is to set realistic goals each
week so you have at least a 70% chance of achieving them.
Success breeds success.

Purpose: Purpose and meaning are important elements of Aging Mastery®. We will suggest many small steps that we think can improve the quality of your life. For each topic and action that we recommend, we try to explain why it matters. We also will encourage you to think more deeply about the big question: What is your purpose in this phase of life?

You want to be in control of your life and be able to do what you want. You want to be as healthy as you can be. You want to have financial security. You want each day to be meaningful and enjoyable.

With these ideas in mind, we've designed Aging Mastery® to help you:

- Make the most of your gift of time.
- Be more aware and intentional about how you spend your time.
- Share your talents with others to make a better world.

SIX DIMENSIONS OF AGING MASTERY®

The experts at the National Council on Aging (NCOA) have worked for more than 65 years to improve the health and well-being of people over the age of 60. While there are many aspects to aging well, we believe that there are six key dimensions. Others may approach the dimensions of aging well differently, but these six work for us—and we hope they will work for you as well.

The Aging Mastery® Six Dimensions of Aging Well

We believe it is very important that people make progress across all six dimensions. As you read through the materials, you will probably find yourself attracted to certain dimensions more than others. Feel free to start wherever feels comfortable to you. But keep in mind that the dimensions you are avoiding may very well be the ones that are most important to tackle.

As part of these six dimensions, we created a set of **Aging Mastery® Guideposts**. These benchmarks are points of reference for you in your Aging Mastery® journey as you take the small steps necessary to change your life in significant ways. They are activities that we think are extremely important for you to keep top of mind and do.

The Aging Mastery® Guideposts certainly do not cover every aspect of every person's life. However, we believe that the more you incorporate these guideposts into your life as daily practices, the better you'll develop habits across the six dimensions of aging well. Daily practices are those practices that will enable you to be mindful of your time each day and, also, help you incorporate your new behaviors into your daily routine. The end result—we hope—is that you are doing some essential activities on a daily basis, activities such as expressing gratitude, making connections with others, staying active, learning something new, and doing good for others.

(You'll find Aging Mastery® Guideposts listed at the end of each dimension of aging well in **Section II.** In addition, the complete set of Aging Mastery® Guideposts is located at the end of **Section III.**)

We all know that longevity alone does not guarantee aging well and that our circumstances can change from year to year. We believe strongly, though, that adopting positive behavior changes across the six dimensions can put you on the path toward realizing the potential of the gift of a longer life.

1.2 A PLAYBOOK FOR YOU

Which path will you choose?

A BRIEF HISTORY OF AGING MASTERY®

In 2012, the seeds of Aging Mastery® were planted. It started—as many innovations do—with a question: Why isn't there a playbook for baby boomers and older adults as they age?

Jim Firman, president and CEO of the National Council on Aging (NCOA), found himself asking this question. As someone who was approaching the magic age of 65 himself, and having devoted his entire working life to improving the lives of older adults, he realized that this vital question needed a solution. He set out to design, develop, implement, and test a program that would provide that solution. In collaboration with his colleagues and several senior centers, he created the Aging Mastery Program® (AMP). AMP is a 10-part program offered in community centers across the country.

GETTING TO MASTERY

Aging Mastery® means developing the skills and knowledge to make the most of the gift of longevity. Aging Mastery® is achieved by developing sustainable behaviors across many areas of life that will lead to improved

> *"The journey of a thousand miles begins with one step."*
> — *Lao Tzu*

health, stronger financial security, enhanced well-being, and increased societal participation.

Mastery is a process that incorporates both **learning and doing** as shown in the diagram below that is inspired by the work of B.J. Fogg[7], a leader in the field of behavior design.

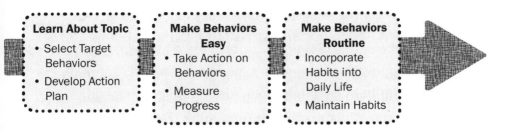

Learn About Topic
- Select Target Behaviors
- Develop Action Plan

Make Behaviors Easy
- Take Action on Behaviors
- Measure Progress

Make Behaviors Routine
- Incorporate Habits into Daily Life
- Maintain Habits

Turning learning into action

Throughout this playbook, you'll learn how to create and maintain habits. In many respects, getting to mastery is all about the thoughtful accumulation of healthy habits that add up to an overall optimal quality of life. Our goal is to provide you with the information, inspiration, and activities you need you to build lifelong habits.

Start small and take small steps.

Habits don't happen overnight: They are the product of slow and steady reinforcement and repetition. And while it's hard to create and reinforce a habit, you're not alone in your journey. You've got your guide (that's us) and you've got your team—all the people in your life, from family to friends to health care providers, who are there to help you along the way.

MAKE IT PERSONAL

The path to mastery is entirely individual. There are no wholly prescriptive rules to follow. Mastery comes when you set a goal, take actions toward that goal, and maintain behaviors necessary to achieve it. For example, in the realm of physical activity, you might set different goals depending on your current level of activity and your abilities. Walking more and lifting small weights might work for some, while training for a 5K and actively doing strength training might be appropriate for others. Whatever your level of physical activity is now, set a stretch goal to be more physically fit. The important part is to take the **first step**.

This playbook is your guide to Aging Mastery®. In these pages, you won't find an encyclopedia for aging well. Rather, you'll find information and inspiration for remaining positively engaged in life. You'll be prompted to think about what you can do to make the most of your gift of time. We'll give you the guideposts, but you need to chart your own course.

As you get ready to set off, here are some guiding principles to ensure a smooth journey:

- **Your path, your goals**. We'll give you inspiration and push you to step out of your comfort zone, but it's important that you set your own goals and make them meaningful to you. Not only will you be more likely to achieve them, but you'll reap outsize rewards.
- **Focus on the outcome**. There will be plenty of bumps and zig-zags on your path to Aging Mastery®. The key is remembering why you're doing this and being open to making mistakes, embracing your imperfections, and continuing forward.
- **Mix it up**. Choose activities and goals that are easy for you so you get some early "wins," but also mix it up with stretch goals that are more difficult. Challenge yourself to focus on areas of your life that you often let fall by the wayside.
- **Embrace the silences**. Our pursuit of a goal does not always mean continual positive reinforcement. Sometimes, long periods of silence—where no real effect is seen—happen. Don't be discouraged. Change will happen. And setting daily practices will help.
- **Be aware of your drivers**. Many of your goals will be challenging, which is why it's helpful to understand what motivates you. Tangible rewards? Outside acknowledgment? The satisfaction of personal achievement? Think carefully about what motivates you to achieve your goals in each dimension of aging well.
- **Share your journey**. Once you have your list of drivers, think about how you can apply them to your goals in real ways. Recruit friends and family to be your companions on your path to Aging Mastery®. Share goals with them, and give them weekly updates on your progress. Support is crucial—and also adds to the fun!

YOUR AGING MASTERY® TEAM

It's your life, and you call the plays. Who's on your Aging Mastery® team to support you? What roles do they play?

Think about the people around you, and put together a lineup for your Aging Mastery® team. Think about your core players. These are the people you turn to on a daily or weekly basis who provide you with emotional support, advice, and companionship. This group might include close friends, significant others, kids (or grandkids), or siblings.

Next, you've got your specialists. These are members of your team whom you call on for specific needs, such as health care assistance, spiritual advice, or exercise motivation. Maybe you have a friend you call up when you need to laugh, or a monthly book club that keeps you intellectually stimulated, or a nurse you trust for between-appointment advice.

Finally, don't forget your other fans out there! Even if you don't interact with them daily, there's a huge group of people out there—in your community, extended family, and work life—rooting for you to succeed on your path to Aging Mastery®.

As you read this playbook and learn more about Aging Mastery®, keep your team in mind. You can even visualize or write down your key lineup. These are the people with whom you can share your learnings, your speed bumps, and your progress.

Your team gives you support, advice, and companionship.

JOIN THE JOURNEY!

Let's start your Aging Mastery® journey.

Along the way, we'll want you to consider some questions: What do you plan to do with the rest of your life? What are your goals? How are you spending your time? What are you looking forward to? Are you prepared for the future? Why are you here?

Growing older doesn't have to be overwhelming or depressing. Despite the challenges that you will face, this can be the best time of your life. Remember, this is a marathon—designed by you—not a sprint. By pursuing Aging Mastery®, you are not only helping yourself but helping to blaze the trail for others to follow.

THE SIX DIMENSIONS OF AGING WELL

2.1 GRATITUDE AND MINDFULNESS

Gratitude is unique to you. The actual things for which you are grateful may change from day to day, but the way you approach gratitude will be constant. Gratitude comes when we focus on what we have and can be thankful for, rather than what we don't have (and maybe do not even need).

Appreciating the world around us from the moment we wake up until the moment we go to sleep is a skill to be learned and incorporated into daily living. It is the starting point of aging both masterfully and gracefully.

THE IMPORTANCE OF GRATITUDE

Gratitude grounds us in life and nudges us to be always mindful of our place in the world. Moreover, various studies[8-11] have shown that gratitude has a uniquely powerful relationship with health and well-being, both our own and of others around us. When people have higher levels of gratitude, they tend to be more socially connected, better able to handle stress, have lower levels of depression, better sleep quality, and stronger biomarkers such as higher rates of good cholesterol.

> *"Gratitude is the affirmation that there are good things in the world, gifts and benefits we've received … an acknowledgment that other people—or even higher powers, if you're of a spiritual mindset—give us many gifts, big and small to help us achieve goodness in our lives."*
>
> *— Robert Emmons, Greater Good Science Center*

By practicing gratitude over time, we can learn to notice and appreciate not only the things that are going well in our lives but also develop better attitudes about the "negative" things, potentially changing those negatives to positives.

For example, as we age, we experience losses and everyday annoyances that can frustrate us or make us sad, angry, or even resentful. When things are going well in our lives, it can be relatively easy to express gratitude on a daily basis. Gratitude truly does come naturally, whether we express it outwardly or not. However, when things are not going so well, expressing gratitude can become more of a challenge. Adopting an attitude of gratitude means tackling the negative things and challenging ourselves to find ways to be grateful for them.

AMPlify Your Thinking

Watch the Louis Schwartzberg TED Talk "Gratitude": https://youtu.be/gXDMoiEkyuQ

What insight did you take away from this video? What is one thing that you are especially grateful for? What are some things that you take for granted every day?

You can express gratitude in a multitude of ways—there is no one-size-fits-all approach—but practice does make perfect. Writing thank-you notes to people who have made a difference in your life is a great place to start. Maybe you want to be more intentional about thanking people as you go about your daily routine. If you're the type of person who prefers to show rather than tell, make a small gift for someone who has helped you out, whether it was recently or several years back. It's never too late to show gratitude.

You may prefer to express your gratitude in a more introspective way by keeping a journal. Gratitude journals are a very effective way of both expressing gratitude and marking important occasions in your life. A journal helps you watch your blessings accumulate over time which can be a source of both inspiration and solace in your life. As you reflect on and write down the things you are grateful for, also consider what your life would be like if these things did not exist or you lost them.

TIPS
- Jot down a few things every week for which you are especially grateful.
- Send a personalized thank-you card to someone special in your life.

The more that you incorporate gratitude into your daily life, the more natural it will become.

FOCUSING ON MINDFULNESS

Mindfulness is an approach to living that focuses on how we experience the world and the mindset that we bring to these experiences. Mindfulness has

"I have arrived. I am home. My destination is in each step."

— Thich Nhat Hanh

very specific meanings in Buddhism, and a long and rich history of practices associated with it. In this section, we will explore what mindfulness means in the context of Aging Mastery® and the central role that gratitude plays in this phase of life.

WHY PRACTICE MINDFULNESS?

When it comes to maintaining or improving our overall health, we often think only about activities we can do to improve our physical health. When we walk, we strengthen our heart and tone our muscles. When we lift weights or do yoga, we increase our bone density. When we ride bikes, we help our circulation.

But how often do you think about exercising your mind and incorporating that exercise as part of your daily routine? In Aging Mastery®, exercising your mind does not mean doing the daily crossword puzzle. (Though there is nothing wrong with that!) Exercising your mind means bringing mindfulness into your life and practicing it on a daily basis, or as often as you can.

Why is mindfulness so important in Aging Mastery®? Mindfulness is central to improving mental and physical health, for building positive habits, and for strengthening your decision-making autonomy.

Many studies[12-15] point to a connection between mindfulness and better overall health, particularly psychological health. When people practice mindfulness basics—such as conscious awareness of actions, living in the present, and nonjudgmental acceptance—stress levels, anxiety, fear, and worries can all be reduced. Some research related to mindfulness has focused specifically on older adults and shown beneficial impact. In one study, mindfulness meditation reduced feelings of loneliness among older adults— an important finding when we know that isolation can have a cascading negative effect on a person's health.

Mindfulness also puts us on the path to **building the positive habits** necessary for mastery in all other dimensions of aging. In a very profound way, mindfulness is a core construct of Aging Mastery®.

In addition to building positive habits, mindfulness can also help us reverse negative habits, a practice that will help you take the journey in all dimensions of aging. Finally, mindfulness helps put us in the driver's seat when we make decisions. It helps to get us to the autonomy that we spoke about in the first section of this book.

It's all about taking small steps. So, let's break mindfulness down step by step.

MINDFULNESS BASICS

Mindfulness is the ability to remain aware, calm, and focused in the present moment.

There are many means to mindfulness. One means is meditation, a mind and body practice that helps increase calmness and physical relaxation, improve psychological balance, and enhance health and well-being.

Learning the basics of meditation isn't difficult. Better yet, it can take as little as 10 minutes a day. A meditation practice that incorporates mindfulness can be as simple as focusing carefully on your breathing, repeating a single word, or visualizing a pleasant object.

Typically, meditation incorporates the following four features[16]:

1. A quiet location with as few distractions as possible.

2. A specific, comfortable posture like sitting, lying down, walking.

3. A point of focus, such as a specially chosen word or set of words, an object, or the sensations of the breath.

4. An open attitude: letting distractions come and go naturally without judgment.

MAKE EACH DAY A MINDFUL DAY

Let's consider some other means to mindfulness that are less structured than formal meditation. For example, there are probably many ways in which you are already incorporating mindfulness in your daily life. Getting absorbed in an activity and giving all of your attention to that activity is mindfulness in action. Maybe it is cooking, or gardening, or woodworking, or walking. We all know that incredible feeling when we are "in the zone" while doing an activity that interests and inspires us.

AMPlify Your Thinking

Maybe you think mindfulness is not for you. We hope to change your perspective on this. Take a moment and read this quote from the investor Warren Buffett:

"I insist on a lot of time being spent, almost every day, to just sit and think. That is very uncommon in American business. I read and think. So, I do more reading and thinking, and make less impulse decisions than most people in business. I do it because I like this kind of life."

Do his daily activities qualify as mindfulness practice? Ask friends what they think. What do you already do every day that helps you make more mindful decisions?

MINDFULNESS AND MEMORY

Mindfulness and memory go hand in hand. Memory is very important to all of us. Our memories shape who we are and our connection to the world. Our memories can be a great ally. We share stories and memories with others, creating a tapestry of our lives and passing on traditions.

At the same time, growing older means that our memories can also become a nagging enemy. Most people notice more memory mistakes as they get older and these mistakes can annoy, frustrate, and even disturb us. Not all memory mistakes can be easily fixed. However, applying mindfulness-style techniques can help reduce memory errors by modifying memory behavior so that we can improve our everyday memory.[17]

Among the memory changes that we notice as we grow older, lack of attention and the ability to learn new things often rise to the top. Paying attention is critical for memory and for learning. If you do not pay attention to a name, a time for a meeting, or where you have parked your car, there is little chance that you will later remember it.

Memory Change = Lack of Attention	What You Can Do About It
It is harder to focus our attention on important things and ignore things in the background. We can be distracted by something on the outside (conversation in the next room) or the inside (thoughts about the next day or the next week). We can lose our place in activities we are doing. All of these changes affect memory.	• Do only one thing at a time. • Stop outside distractions. Turn off the TV or radio and keep others away when you want to do mental work. • Keep a piece of paper handy—make a quick note about any off-topic ideas that come to mind and then concentrate again on what you were doing. • To focus your attention on something you want to remember, describe it, make a mental picture, or think about what it means to you.

Memory Change = New Learning Challenges	What You Can Do About It
With age, it often takes longer to master something new. It also takes more effort to learn. We may need to review new information four or five times before we know it. Things don't stick as easily as they did when we were younger.	• Be prepared to make an effort when you want to remember something new. • Review new items many times. • Personal meaning strengthens memory, so connect your new item to your life—your knowledge, your feelings, your experience. • Stay mentally active. The more you use your brain on real-world memory activities, the better it will work for you.

You will remember more if you use a mindfulness-style technique called Active Attention in your everyday life. Active Attention is a method used for remembering pictures, events, or scenes. The idea is for you to focus your attention completely on a scene in front of you. You want to notice the central aspects of the scene and important details.

Active Attention requires you to focus your mind. People commonly turn off their minds when they are tending to normal daily activities. For example, when setting aside your glasses, you may not pay attention to where you put them. As you get older, you may have a tendency to do this more often. Instead of allowing such absentmindedness to take over, you should take note of what you are doing, seeing, and hearing by using Active Attention. For example, you could say to yourself, "I am taking off my glasses and setting them next to the bed so they will be there in the morning." When you are mindful about your actions and your surroundings, remembering them becomes easier.

AMPlify Your Behavior

Practice Active Attention

1. Recall where you have put something by closing your eyes and picturing nearby objects.

2. Remember things you have done by focusing on what you were wearing or something specific that happened that day.

3. Recollect an event by attending to the details when you go to the event. Experience it fully. Look around you and describe the scene to yourself.

4. Recall a person by noticing facial features, hair, and glasses when you meet them.

WRAP-UP: YOUR AMP GRATITUDE AND MINDFULNESS GUIDEPOSTS

 Use the following guideposts to encourage optimal behaviors related to gratitude and mindfulness. If you are already doing these activities, super! If you are not doing these activities, think about ways that you can set goals and change your behaviors. Remember that the guideposts are markers for your Aging Mastery® journey. Your personal situation and abilities will impact how you incorporate these activities into your life.

Gratitude and Mindfulness Guideposts

	How often?
I write down three things that I am grateful for.	Daily
I meditate for 10 minutes.	Daily
I notice and appreciate something small and wonderful.	Daily
I am accountable and responsible for my actions.	Daily
I set goals for each day.	Daily
I reflect on my progress toward my goals.	Daily
I express gratitude to people who make a difference in my life.	Weekly
I focus on changing unwanted habits.	Weekly

SELECTED RESOURCES: GRATITUDE AND MINDFULNESS
Websites and Other Media
Greater Good Science Center: www.greatergood.berkeley.edu

Helpguide.org, "Benefits of Mindfulness":
www.helpguide.org/harvard/benefits-of-mindfulness.htm

Helpguide.org, "Relaxation Techniques for Stress Relief":
www.helpguide.org/articles/stress/relaxation-techniques-for-stress-relief.htm

National Center for Complementary and Integrative Health, "Meditation-In Depth":
www.nccih.nih.gov/health/meditation/overview.htm

MindBody Lab: www.cmhc.utexas.edu/mindbodylab.html

Andy Puddicombe, "All it takes is 10 mindful minutes":
www.ted.com/speakers/andy_puddicombe

Louie Schwartzberg, "Nature, Beauty, Gratitude":
www.ted.com/speakers/louie_schwartzberg

Sitting Together: www.sittingtogether.com/meditations.php

THNX4: www.thnx4.org

UCLA Mindful Awareness Research Center:
www.marc.ucla.edu/body.cfm?id=22

2.2 HEALTH AND WELL-BEING

The key to good health might be closer than you think.

Health is an important foundation of aging masterfully. If your health falters—if you are ill, fatigued, in pain, anxious, or depressed—you will find it very difficult to make the most of your gift of longevity, and your overall quality of life will suffer.

Your health and well-being workout needs to be a comprehensive routine. Eating right and exercising regularly are givens. But you also need to pay attention to sleep, hydration, injury prevention, and your medical needs. We've constructed an Aging Mastery® Health and Well-Being workout as a cycle made up of these elements:

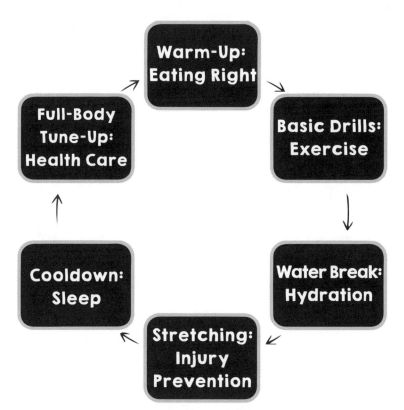

Your health and well-being workout

As you look at the diagram and read more about each of these elements, keep in mind what Aristotle once said: "The whole is greater than the sum of its parts." Each element by itself is important; together, they are much more powerful. The opposite is also true: If you remove one element, the whole will suffer. For example, removing hydration from your health and well-being workout could expose you to a constellation of medical problems that would have a detrimental impact on your overall health.

The workout that follows provides a good basis for you to understand certain best practices for aging well. We recognize that the workout is not comprehensive and that there are a myriad of topics--such as mental health and sexual health that are not addressed, We hope this selection, though, gives you a solid foundation from which to build a more comprehensive approach to your health and well-being.

WARM-UP: EATING RIGHT

Wherever you are in life, and whatever your motivation, eating healthy and maintaining adequate fluid intake can help you avoid health concerns, increase your longevity, and provide you more quality time to enjoy the things that matter most to you.

> *"It is health that is real wealth and not pieces of gold and silver."*
>
> — *Mahatma Gandhi*

Good eating habits not only give you more energy and endurance, but also play an important role in preventing major causes of illness and death, including heart disease, cancer, diabetes, and obesity. Good nutrition provides the calories you need to fuel your days. It helps enhance your body's strength, flexibility, balance, and endurance by keeping muscles, bones, and joints stronger and in better shape.

Moreover, a balanced and nutritious diet can help you recover from an injury, illness, or surgery. And, if you do get a serious medical condition such as heart disease, hypertension, stroke, diabetes, bone loss, or anemia, these conditions can all benefit from a balanced, nutritious diet. Finally, good nutrition has a positive impact on your appearance, which can affect your self-esteem, mental health, and social life.

Guiding Principles for Good Eating Habits

The world of nutrition can often seem complicated. A week doesn't go by when a new study about food is released that appears to contradict a prior study. Moreover, the many scientific explanations of nutrition and the vast array of diet plans can be overwhelming. It's no wonder that many of us turn a deaf ear to any new study related to nutrition. By this point in our lives, we've likely tried a diet or two, or hopped on a trendy food bandwagon.

No one nutritional approach is the silver bullet for all of us. Medical conditions, medications, food preferences, access to food, etc., all play a role in our daily diets. However, there are some basic principles of healthy eating for older adults that have stood the test of time. Use these five principles as your guideposts as you think about your own eating habits.

Five Principles for Good Nutrition[18]

1	**Exercise moderation** That whole pint of ice cream or bowl of peanuts might be tempting, but a smaller serving is the better choice. In all your food and beverage choices, aim for moderation rather than excess. Read nutrition labels, follow recommended servings, and actively choose foods with less fat, added sugars, and sodium.
2	**Choose nutrient-rich foods** Concentrate your meals around proteins, fruits, vegetables, whole grains, nuts and legumes, and low-fat dairy. They may help you control your weight, cholesterol, and blood pressure. ChooseMyPlate.gov recommends that older adults make half of each meal fruits and vegetables.

3	**Build a colorful plate** Indulge your senses! Make your food look beautiful by adding color and variety to your plate. While you're at it, decrease the size of the plates and bowls you use to help with portion control.
4	**Avoid empty calories and added sugar** A calorie is a calorie, so make each calorie count. Focus on calories that both sustain you and energize your body in the long term, not just calories that fill you up in the short term. An easy way to do this is to cut back on beverages and foods with added sugars, as well as caloric snacks such as chips, pretzels, and crackers.
5	**Limit bad fats and sodium** Open your cupboard or fridge. Put your monounsaturated and polyunsaturated fats (olive oil, sunflower oil, etc.) to the front and your saturated and trans fats (butter, shortening, margarine, partially hydrogenated oil, etc.) to the back and limit their use. Partially hydrogenated oils lurk everywhere from baked goods and non-dairy creamers to chips, fried foods of all kinds, and refrigerator dough products. Also, choose foods with less sodium, and prepare foods with as little salt as possible.

According to the National Institute on Aging, a moderately active woman over age 50 should consume about 1,800 calories a day to stay at her current weight.[19] For an older man, that number is 2,200 to 2,400. (Moderate activity is defined as 30 minutes of exercise, five days a week.) Practicing good nutrition involves getting the right amount of the basic nutrients that your body needs to function properly and prevent or fight disease.

Take some time to think about what determines the way you eat. Put a checkmark next to the 2–3 items that either motivate or limit the way you eat the most.

My Eating Drivers	✓
Finances (how much food costs)	
Convenience (what food I have on hand)	
Taste (what food tastes like)	
Emotions (what mood I'm in)	
Habits (what I'm used to cooking/eating)	
Accessibility (how easy is it to get to the store)	
Loss of appetite	
Health and medications (how these affect food choices)	
Other? (for example, preferences of other family members)	

Of these items, which ones have the most impact on the way you eat? Is the impact a positive or a negative one? Are there drivers that you'd like to change? How can you make that change happen?

Eat With Good Sense—and Gusto!

Many of us fall into mindless eating and get stuck in poor eating patterns. We reach for the foods that are at hand or choose packaged foods that don't require much preparation. These patterns can be detrimental not only to our health, but also to the experience of pleasure that should come with eating. Living to eat and enjoying what we eat should always take priority over simply eating to live as long as it's within our means.

As much as you are able, we want to encourage you to eat with **gusto**. The word "gusto" comes from the Latin word *gustus*, or taste/tasting. It seems common sense to say that taste should be the focal point of our eating, but the realities of growing older sometimes get in the way of common sense. As we age, we may experience decreased appetite and decreased mobility or have limited access to healthy food, among other challenges. There are times when we may not want or be able to eat a full meal. Maybe food no longer tastes that good at all (because of a medication), we get full fast, or we're simply not interested in eating. Living alone can also profoundly change the way we eat and cause us to limit the variety of food we buy for ourselves.

The cost of health care and medications can also put such a dent in our income that we forego buying food in favor of making sure we get our medications. Finally, a bodily change that inhibits the ability to chew or swallow can severely disrupt our eating patterns and our desire to enjoy food.

How can we make up for some of the factors that prevent us from eating with gusto? Three words: **snacking**, **spicing**, and **socializing**. Including healthy, small snacks throughout the day will help ensure you get key nutrients in your diet. Adding herbs and spices makes food taste good, can cut down on the desire for salty foods, and can restore flavor to bland foods. Making mealtime a social activity is both fun and encourages you change up your routine. Plus, it can save on food expenses if everyone brings a favorite dish. Invite a friend or loved one to lunch, or organize a potluck with several friends and neighbors.

Eating with gusto is not just about getting enjoyment out of food. It is also about good sense. Older adults are particularly vulnerable and at risk for malnutrition which is an imbalance of the nutrients you need to stay healthy. Diets low in calories can lead to malnutrition, but so can a diet high in calories. For example, if your diet is high in calories, but low in key vitamins and minerals, you might become malnourished. Malnutrition matters because it increases risks for serious health problems. Malnourished individuals suffer from weakened immune systems (resulting sometimes in increased infections), difficulty staying warm, poor wound healing, and longer recoveries. In addition, many people experience issues like loss of appetite, which only makes the problem worse.

Malnutrition and loss of muscle or lean body mass also often go hand in hand. Combined with poor eating, these two factors can create a domino effect that both increases our likelihood of developing malnutrition and aggravates malnutrition symptoms. Muscle loss makes us lose strength, impairs our mobility, and decreases our ability to do basic activities such as standing up or opening a door. These factors increase the risk of falling and put us at risk for not getting the right nutrients, such as when lack of mobility prevents us from going to the grocery store.

TIPS

If you're living on a fixed income, you may be able to get help paying for healthy food and stretch your food budget. Visit NCOA's free www.BenefitsCheckUp.org/getSNAP to learn more.

Our body and nutrient needs change as we get older, and as our health status changes, so it's especially important to make sure that we pay attention to what we eat to get adequate amounts of fluids, protein, calcium, and vitamin D. Adding exercise to the nutrition equation helps complete part of the equation to keeping our bones strong and muscles nimble.

BASIC DRILLS: EXERCISE

Now that your body has the fuel it needs, you can begin to think about your exercise routine. Basic guidelines, from organizations such as the World Health Organization[20] (WHO), tell us that we should engage in moderate physical activity for at least 30 minutes a day five days a week and muscle-strengthening activities that work all major muscle groups on two or more days each week.

As with all things Aging Mastery®, you'll want to make your exercise routine your own by following these basic guidelines and then tailoring them to your abilities and capacities. The important thing is to develop a schedule and stick to it as best as possible. If it's hard to schedule regular exercise sessions, try aiming for shorter sessions of at least 10 minutes each spread throughout the week. If you get bored easily, try something new! Ask friends about new exercise programs or go online and watch a video of a new type of exercise that you've read about. Doing so may inspire you to find a class nearby. Another great option is to enlist a friend or two and become exercise buddies together. You will hold yourself more accountable when you exercise as a team. Most of all, enjoy yourself! Exercise invigorates the body and the mind.

The Starting Block: Endurance, Strength, Balance, and Flexibility

Because muscle loss and mobility issues can occur as we age, the basic guidelines focus on aerobics, strength, flexibility, and balance. Keep in mind that no matter how much or how little you are doing now, there is always room for improvement. For example, you can do a little more than you were doing or add a new exercise element to your routine. Don't think of exercise as a competition against others or even against yourself. Exercising helps you attain the best health you can achieve given your current circumstances—full stop.

Create a routine that combines the four basic types of physical exercise as recommended by the National Institute on Aging's Go4Life website.[21] Many recreation and community centers offer regular classes as well as low or no-cost advice from personal trainers to help you build a routine that is appropriate for you.

Endurance—These are also known as "aerobic" or "cardio" exercises. They cause your heart and breathing rate to increase, improving cardio, circulatory, and pulmonary functions. Endurance exercises may also build strength. Examples include vigorous walking, jogging, yard work, and dancing.

Strength—The primary focus of these exercises is to build your muscles. They are often called "strength training" or "resistance training." Examples include weight lifting, exercising with resistance bands, or using your body to create resistance.

Balance—As the name suggests, these exercises improve the body's balance to prevent falls. Lower body strengthening exercise also helps you maintain balance. Examples include standing on one foot, walking heel-to-toe, and Tai Chi.

Flexibility—These are also known as "stretching" exercises. They can improve your body's freedom of movement by stretching your muscles. Examples include upper-arm stretches, calf stretches, and other exercise routines such as yoga.

Adapted from www.go4life.nia.nih.gov.

Before beginning or altering your exercise routine, consult your health care team. Your health care providers can advise you on appropriate exercise based on your health history. If you have a prior heart condition or are on blood pressure medication, your health care provider can give you an appropriate heart rate range for exercise. Regularly assess your physical activities and ensure that your physical activity program is correct based on your current health.

AMPlify Your Behavior

Does your exercise routine cover all four areas of endurance, strength, balance, and flexibility?

- If your answer is **No**, take steps this week to research new exercise routines that can help you fill in those blank spots.

- If your answer is **Yes**, take steps this week to change up one exercise in one of the four areas. For example, if you normally do weight lifting for strength, try using resistance bands instead.

WATER BREAK: HYDRATION

Quick test. **True or False:**

1. Thirst perception declines as you age.

2. The ability to conserve water is reduced as you age.

3. Medications and chronic conditions can inhibit the desire or ability to drink fluids.

If you answered True to all three statements, you're correct. Any of these factors can lead to dehydration which can then lead to a host of other issues. Dehydration puts you at risk for poor mental function, infectious diseases, renal disease, and constipation. In addition, it is one of the 10 most frequent diagnoses leading to hospitalization. Living alone or in a care home can also increase chances of dehydration. These factors can be compounded by chronic illnesses such as diabetes, kidney disease, heart failure, and dementia.

Dehydration can sneak up on you. That's why proper hydration is a prerequisite for your health and well-being workout.

AMPlify Your Behavior

Even if you think you are drinking enough, be mindful of your daily dose of fluids:

- Take sips from a glass of water, milk, or juice between bites during meals.
- Drink a full glass of water if you need to take a pill.
- Have a glass of water before you exercise or go outside to garden or walk.
- Drink fat-free or low-fat milk, or other drinks without added sugars.
- If you drink alcoholic beverages, do so sensibly and in moderation. That means up to one drink per day for women and up to two drinks for men. Check with your doctor about how much alcohol is safe for you to drink as certain medications interact with alcohol.
- Don't stop drinking liquids if you have a urinary control problem. Talk with your doctor about treatment.

Adapted from *Drinking Enough Fluids* www.nia.nih.gov/Go4Life

STRETCHING: INJURY PREVENTION

Stretching at the end of any exercise routine helps realign your body and helps you avoid injury. Your Aging Mastery® stretch will bring the same benefits. This particular stretch is all about taking the necessary steps to prevent falls and thus avoid injuries that can severely impact your ability to move about independently.

The statistics on falls-related injuries are sobering. 1 in 4 older Americans falls every year and 1 out of 5 of these falls causes a serious injury. 2.5 million older people are treated in emergency departments for fall injuries. Falls are the leading cause of both fatal and nonfatal injuries for people aged 65+. Falls can result in hip fractures, broken bones, and head injuries. And even falls without a major injury can cause you to become fearful or depressed, making it difficult to stay active.

That's the not-so-good news. The better news is that most falls are also preventable. Following six basic guidelines will help you move with confidence and care.

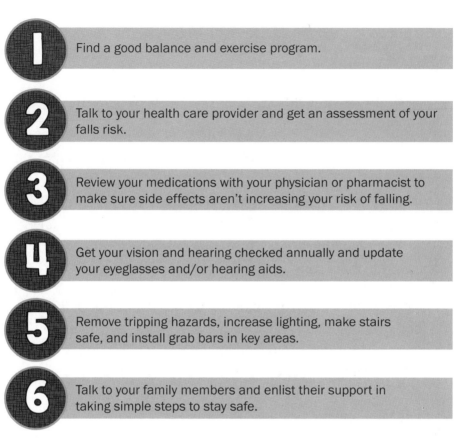

1. Find a good balance and exercise program.

2. Talk to your health care provider and get an assessment of your falls risk.

3. Review your medications with your physician or pharmacist to make sure side effects aren't increasing your risk of falling.

4. Get your vision and hearing checked annually and update your eyeglasses and/or hearing aids.

5. Remove tripping hazards, increase lighting, make stairs safe, and install grab bars in key areas.

6. Talk to your family members and enlist their support in taking simple steps to stay safe.

Six steps to prevent a fall[22]

Getting Past Misconceptions About Falls

Misconception #1: Falling is something normal that happens as we get older.
Falling is not a normal part of aging. Strength and balance exercises, managing your medications, having your vision and hearing checked, and making your living environment safer are all steps you can take to prevent a fall.

Misconception #2: If I limit my activity, I won't fall.
Performing physical activities will help you stay independent as your strength and range of motion benefit from remaining active. Social activities are also good for your overall health.

Misconception #3: Muscle strength and flexibility cannot be regained.

While we do lose muscle as we age, exercise can partially restore strength and flexibility. Start an exercise program and increase your physical activity.

Misconception #4: Using a walker or cane will make me more dependent.

Walking aids are very important in helping us maintain or improve our mobility. Make sure you use these devices safely. Have a physical therapist fit the walker or cane to you and instruct you in its safe use.

Misconception #5: As long as I stay at home, I can avoid falling.
In fact, over half of all falls take place at home, so you are more likely to fall at home than outside. Inspect your home for fall risks. Fix simple but serious hazards such as clutter, throw rugs, and poor lighting, and make needed home modifications to ensure your safety.[23]

Taking Corrective Steps to Fall-Proof Your Home

Look around you. Are there papers, books, towels, shoes, or other objects on the floor? Are many of your cupboards out of reach? Is your bathroom, kitchen, or bedroom a tangle of wires? Are you missing a light in a hallway, stairway, or other essential location? Now is the time to do a complete home safety check, particularly if you have fallen in the past year or feel unsteady when you walk. The following table highlights some hotspots for falls in the home and presents simple and inexpensive ways to make your home safer.

Home Safety Check[24]

Obstructed Pathways and Area Rugs	<ul><li>Remove and relocate any clutter, furniture, or exposed electrical wires.</li><li>If you use a mobility device, allow for at least 36 inches of clear-width pathway throughout your home for ease of mobility.</li><li>Remove throw rugs to maintain smooth, even walking surfaces.</li><li>If throw rugs remain, ensure that they do not move and that corners will not curl. Choose rugs that have heavy rubber underlays or use double-sided tape.</li></ul>
Steps and Handrails	<ul><li>Pull carpet tight to smooth out ripples and avoid tripping.</li><li>Install a slip-resistant rough finish on stair treads, especially for stairs that can get wet.</li><li>Mark landings and stair edges (nosings) by painting or staining a contrasting color stripe on the nosing of each tread for visibility. Do not use tape.</li><li>Have light switches at the tops and bottoms of stairways.</li><li>Have uniform lighting in stairways and surrounding areas.</li><li>Install continuous handrails on both sides of stairways, extending 1 foot beyond the top and bottom steps.</li></ul>

Lighting	• Increase task lighting. • Replace dim bulbs with brighter, more efficient bulbs. (If you have an eye condition such as macular degeneration, glaucoma, or cataracts, determine the type of bulb you need.) • Use motion-sensor switches to automatically detect movement and illuminate paths, as well as reduce energy consumption. • Balance light throughout the home to decrease light transitions.
Bathrooms	• Install taller toilets, add raised toilet seats, or use 3-in-1 commode chairs that are height-adjustable and can be placed directly over the existing toilets. • Add grab bars near toilets and within shower/tub areas to assist with the motion of sitting to standing. • Sit (rather than stand) while showering. • Use a handheld showerhead to minimize reaching and to increase access to water. • Use a non-skid bathmat or bath strips in the tub. • Avoid using bath oils and lotions that can make surfaces slippery. • Wear wet shoes for more grip on the floor when stepping in or out of the shower/tub.

If you have a medical condition, consider consulting an occupational therapist to make recommendations tailored to your personal needs. Occupational therapists look at your specific environment, understand how you live, and assess individual factors (such as mobility) that might impact the way you move about your environment.

COOLDOWN: SLEEP

Sleep helps keep us healthier, stronger, and more alert while helping the body to repair cell and organ damage that occurs during the day. All good things. The flip side of the coin is not so rosy. When we do not sleep well, we may suffer from depression, attention and memory problems, and excessive daytime sleepiness. We are also likely to experience nighttime falls, increased sensitivity to pain, and the need to use more prescription or over-the-counter sleep aids. Finally, lack of sleep may contribute to health problems including a greater risk of cardiovascular disease, diabetes, weight problems, and breast cancer in women.[25]

> ### The Optimal Cooldown
> Most of us need 7.5 to 9 hours of sleep every night. However, the number of hours you are asleep is not as important as how you feel following a good night's sleep. For example, if you have always functioned well on 6 hours of sleep and that remains your sleep pattern, then 6 hours is likely your optimal cooldown.

The Age/Sleep Equation

There's a common belief that we need less sleep as we age. That's not true. Our sleep needs are consistent throughout adulthood. What changes are our sleep patterns, making it likely that we'll have a more difficult time falling asleep, staying asleep, or experiencing that really good deep sleep.

More fragmented sleep[26] is typical as we get older as are the urges to fall sleep earlier in the evening and to wake up earlier in the morning. These changes arise partly from hormonal and circadian rhythm changes, and can significantly interrupt sustained sleep. Also, many health conditions (such as asthma, heartburn, and menopause) interfere with our ability to get a good night's sleep as do pain, stress, depression, medications, and sleep disorders.

Changing Up Routines for Better Sleep

As with many aspects of our lives, there are things that we cannot control and other things we can control. We cannot, for example, reverse hormonal changes. However, many barriers to a good night's sleep are self-imposed and within our ability to change them. They're just bad habits and, as we've learned, changing habits takes commitment and small steps.

Poor sleep habits—including a poor sleep environment and poor daytime habits—can be the main cause of sleep problems and low-quality sleep. Often, we develop these habits over a lifetime but find they create more and more problems as we age. Fortunately, these habits are often easy to improve. The following table lists steps you can take to mitigate sleep problems and get the good night's rest that your body needs.

☼ Daytime Habits for Better Sleep[27]	☾ Nighttime Habits for Better Sleep
Exercise regularly.	Turn devices off: radio, TV, phone, etc.
Talk about your worries with a friend.	Reduce artificial light as much as possible.
Stay engaged socially.	Limit noise and heat in your bedroom.
Get sunlight.	Keep a regular bedtime routine.
Limit caffeine, alcohol, and nicotine especially in the afternoon and evening.	Do not read from a backlit device.
Avoid big meals and late-night snacks before bedtime.	Use your bedroom for sleep and sex only.

To Nap or Not to Nap

A brief nap can re-energize you enough to be more active and productive the rest of the day. And many believe that we are biologically programmed to sleep twice per day, so a nap helps address this biological need. Where we get into trouble with napping is when we rely on it to help us make up for a nighttime sleep shortfall. In that case, we tend to nap for longer stretches and at the wrong times of the day, such as late afternoon or early evening. If you have a low energy spell or feel sleepy after being awake for several hours, give napping a try and see if it helps. Just remember to nap early in the afternoon and keep the nap to 15–20 minutes. A quick refresh!

When to Call for the Trainer

Although many problems with sleep can be dealt with through simple changes in routine or in the sleep environment, sometimes a change in behavior is not enough. If you are having a particular problem with sleep that goes on for a period of time, consult with your health care team to see if a sleep disorder such as sleep apnea, restless legs syndrome, or narcolepsy, or even your medications, could be interfering with your sleep or if a health problem is the cause.

Keeping a sleep diary will provide much of the information you need to find good solutions. After you and your health team identify the underlying causes of your sleep problem, the next step is to find both long- and short-term solutions. The short-term solutions may require medical treatment along with simple behavioral changes. For longer-term solutions, work to develop a sleep plan and be sure that your plan includes ongoing health-promoting habits such as proper diet, exercise, and stress management strategies.

You spend one-third of your life sleeping. Make the most of your sleep investment so that you can live the other two-thirds in the most energetic, productive, and fulfilling manner possible.

FULL-BODY TUNE-UP: HEALTH CARE

Your health and well-being workout regimen would not be complete without a full-body tune-up. Your Aging Mastery® tune-up should include regular preventive care and tests, annual health visits, and medication management. Staying one step ahead of medical issues is the best way to both prevent them and also to deal with them when they arise.

When we were younger, we probably thought "good health" meant no illness, no chronic conditions, no aches and pains, and so on. As we've gotten older, we've realized that the definition of "good health" is more personal and that even if we have a chronic condition, for example, we may feel in very good health if we can manage the condition properly. The fact is, by this time in our lives, many of us have experienced medical issues that affect our health in one way or the other. Some of us have gone through major illnesses or had surgeries. Others have managed chronic issues for several years. Additionally, those fractures or muscle strains from our earlier years may continue to cause us aches and pains.

So, instead of thinking in terms of good health or perfect health, think in terms of optimal health. Maintaining optimal health means understanding our personal health situations and striving to improve them. Optimal health involves taking care of ourselves, taking our medications as prescribed, and keeping our health care team informed of our stumbles and successes.

Prevention: Still the Best Medicine

Prevention is our first step on the road to optimal health. Preventing diseases before they occur gives us a better chance of living healthier and happier lives, reducing health care costs, and retaining our independence to age in the place of our choice.

Although we do not have the ability to prevent all medical problems, we know it is possible to take steps to avoid many of them. Some of the steps we can all take to help prevent disease include healthy eating, regular exercise, and not smoking.

Another key strategy is to seek out those preventive services that are available to each of us, whether through Medicare, Medicaid, and/or private health insurance. Preventive services include general health assessments, immunizations, lab tests, and disease-specific screenings that can detect problems early and help you stay healthy longer. Education, counseling, and a variety of support programs are also benefits of preventive services. These measures can potentially stop certain diseases and chronic conditions from developing such as heart disease, stroke, and obesity.

Seek prevention services that address all aspects of your physical and emotional well-being. Pay special attention to your five senses, and make sure that you're attending to all of them every year. It can be easy to skip yearly dental or hearing exams, for example, so make sure to mark them on your calendar. Mental health and sexual health are two other areas that often go under the radar either because we hesitate to ask for help or because we are not aware of the preventive services available. Speak directly with your health care team to understand what resources are available to you.

TIPS

www.Medicare.gov and www.MyMedicareMatters.org have comprehensive information on preventive services that are covered by Medicare such as the Annual Wellness visit. Even if you are not on Medicare, these lists provide essential information to help you understand the types of preventive care that you should be seeking out on a regular basis. Talk with your health care team about the preventive services that you need and review this with your team every year.

"But I'm Not Sick": Other Reasons We Avoid Preventive Care

Many of us avoid doctor's visits at all costs—even when the services are part of our health care coverage. We all have our reasons, but avoiding medical care, tests, or immunizations will not make a potential condition go away. The consequences of not getting preventive care can be serious and can actually turn a treatable medical condition into one that is more difficult to treat—or an untreatable one. We all have examples of friends and relatives who either did or did not seek out preventive care. For those who did seek care, the outcomes were life-changing; for those who did not seek care, the consequences could be devastating.

AMPlify Your Thinking

One Aging Mastery® technique is to turn negative thoughts into positive actions. Let's use that approach to think about your reluctance to visit a doctor, dentist, or other health care provider. Read the following avoidance statements and consider how many are true for you.

I am NOT interested in getting preventive services because . . .

- I feel fine and I'm healthy.
- I don't have a doctor (or I don't have a doctor that I like).
- I don't know what my health insurance or benefits cover. I'd rather not go to the doctor at all than be surprised by hidden charges.
- I don't have time to go to the doctor.
- I don't want to be told to change my lifestyle. I don't want to be told what to do.
- I don't want to know if I have a medical condition.
- I don't want to start taking medications.
- I'd rather tough out my aches and pains on my own.
- I don't like being tested for anything.
- I don't have an easy way to get to the doctor.
- I already know my condition. (I'm overweight, I should stop smoking, etc.) Why do I need a doctor to tell me that?

Do you recognize yourself in these avoidance statements? Do you have other avoidance statements of your own? Now, flip the statements on their heads and create a positive action. Here's an example: *I feel fine now, but I can't know everything that's going on in my body. I know that if I want to stay healthy, I need to stay on top of my health and see my health care team.*

The Art of Communication

Another step on our road to optimal health involves how well we communicate with our health care team—and how well that team communicates with us! This is increasingly important especially if our medical needs require us to have multiple health care providers. Often, we are in charge of coordinating many aspects of our own care so communication becomes critical.

You and your health care team should work to make sure that you receive the best care and that they practice good medicine. **A good partnership is based on three important factors: a common goal, shared effort, and good communication.** This means asking questions if you don't understand instructions or explanations, bringing up problems even if your provider doesn't ask, and sharing concerns you may have about changes or treatment plans.

> *"Never go to a doctor whose office plants have died."*
>
> — *Erma Bombeck*

Keys to a successful health visit include doing some prep work upfront and taking notes during the appointment. Make a list of what you want to discuss along with a list of your medications, over-the-counter medicines, vitamins, and herbal remedies. During the visit, write down your diagnosis, the treatment, the follow-up plan, and what you can do at home. If you aren't sure that you can talk, listen, and write at the same time, take a friend or family member along to write down your provider's findings and suggestions. Another idea is to record your doctor visit on a small tape recorder or your phone. That way, you'll have a full record of everything that both you and the doctor have said. Plus, you can share the recording with others in your family. Make sure you understand your diagnosis and its implications. If you don't, have your doctor explain it again and write it down. Share your thoughts or concerns, then come to agreement with your doctor on your treatment options.

AMPlify Your Behavior
Often, health care visits can be stressful. It can be difficult to remember every detail about our health concerns and, more often than not, we don't have nearly enough time to share everything. We can neglect to mention a symptom because we don't feel it's important or remember an important detail the minute we leave the office.

To make the most of your next health care visit, try this: **Act it out ahead of time**. Enlist a friend or family member and talk through everything that you want to discuss. Be as descriptive as possible. Exaggerate your concerns and exaggerate the reactions of your "doctor" friend. Adding a little drama to this role-play will not only help you remember what you want to say, but will also give you the confidence to ask pointed questions so that you get the answers that make sense to you.

Medications and Supplements: Managing the Maze

What one word would sum up your attitude toward medication? Confused? Overwhelmed? Grateful? Relieved? For many of us, it may be one or a combination of these. Growing older sometimes means facing a growing list of health conditions that need to be treated. Medications are not the only way to treat a health condition but are often part of the treatment toolkit. We might wake one day and realize we are taking 5+ medications.

Thus, the third step in your full-body tune-up is management.

Increased use of medications brings with it increased chance of harmful drug interactions. In effect, your body can become a mini-pharmacy. In fact, the term used to describe the simultaneous use of multiple drugs to treat one or more health conditions is polypharmacy. Polypharmacy may occur when several doctors are using a variety of drugs to manage the same or different symptoms. Ideally, your doctors will carefully select, monitor, adjust, and manage the use of two or more medications when treating a single condition or multiple conditions that require multiple drugs. When discussing drugs with health care professionals, always ask about drug interactions. Be sure to mention all prescription medicines and over-the-counter products, including herbal and nutritional supplements that you take.

Managing medications for yourself or for a loved one should always be done in cooperation with your health care team. Your best practice is to regularly review with your doctors all the prescription and non-prescription medications and supplements you take. This review helps your health care team consider possible side effects, drug interactions, or drug sensitivities. If you see multiple doctors, regular medication reviews are even more important. You can also ask your pharmacist for help with your medication questions. Most importantly, if you are concerned by the number of prescriptions that you are taking, be sure to discuss all options with your doctor.

Medication Management in Three Easy Steps

Medication management principles apply to all types of medications: prescription drugs, over-the-counter (OTC) medications, and supplements. Serious medical issues can result from improper use of all types of medications, so it is critical to learn how to store, take, and dispose of your medications safely.

1

Take your medication as prescribed
There are many reasons for not taking medications as prescribed: forgetting; taking the incorrect amount; taking it at the wrong time or for the wrong purpose; not using the right techniques such as inhalers or eye drops; and using drugs prescribed for others. Make sure you understand how to take each of your medications safely. Take it exactly as prescribed, and incorporate this habit into your daily routine.

2

Create a Medication Diary or List
A medication diary can help you with medication adherence. Begin by finding all your medications and containers, putting them in one place, and making a list. Include prescriptions, ointments, eye/ear drops, and OTC medicines such as herbals, supplements, vitamins, minerals, antacids, sleep aids, pain medicine, and laxatives. Include dosages, when taken, and expiration dates, too. Review your medications regularly and update your medication diary accordingly. Keep this diary with you at all times and share it with your doctors.

3

Store and dispose of your medicines safely
Medication should be stored in a cool, dry, dark location. Do no store your medicines in your bathroom. The moisture and heat can degrade them. Create visual reminders for taking your medications, such as syncing with activities such as eating or brushing your teeth. If you live with children or adolescents, or they visit you frequently, you may want to lock up your medications.

Discard any expired medications. Put everything that is current and usable in one pile or box and expired medication in another. (If you are not sure whether a medication has expired, err on the side of safety.) The best way to dispose of medications is through a drug take-back program in your community. Check with your pharmacy about drug take-back programs. If you don't have one nearby, you can mix medicines (do not crush tablets or capsules) with an unpalatable substance such as dirt, kitty litter, or used coffee grounds, then dispose of it in the trash.

WRAP-UP: YOUR AMP HEALTH AND WELL-BEING GUIDEPOSTS

 Use the following guideposts to encourage optimal behaviors related to your health and well-being. If you are already doing these activities, super! If you are not doing these activities, think about ways that you can set goals and change your behaviors. Remember that the guideposts are markers for your Aging Mastery® journey. Your personal situation and abilities will impact how you incorporate these activities into your life.

Health and Well-Being Guideposts

	How often?
I exercise for 30 minutes doing a mix of aerobics, balance, strengthening, and flexibility.	4–5 days/ week
I eat a variety of foods that are nutrient-rich.	Daily
I drink plenty of water and clear liquids.	Daily
I use sleep strategies to maintain consistent sleep.	Daily
I take medications, OTCs, and supplements as directed.	Daily
I keep my home free from hazards that could cause a fall or injury.	Daily
I practice proactive, preventive health care.	Daily
I encourage and support others to help them achieve their health and well-being goals.	Weekly

SELECTED RESOURCES: HEALTH AND WELL-BEING
Book
Dan Buettner: *The Blue Zones: 9 Lessons for Living Longer From the People Who've Lived the Longest*

Websites and Other Media
AGS BEERS Criteria for Potentially Inappropriate Medication Use in Older Adults: www.americangeriatrics.org/files/documents/beers/PrintableBeersPocketCard.pdf

Choose My Plate: www.choosemyplate.gov

Environmental Protection Agency, "How to Dispose of Medicines Properly":
www.epa.gov/sites/production/files/2015-06/documents/how-to-dispose-medicines.pdf

Food and Drug Administration, "Medicines and You: A Guide for Older Adults": www.fda.gov/downloads/Drugs/ResourcesForYou/UCM163961.pdf

Go4Life: www.go4life.nia.nih.gov

Helpguide.org, "Sleep Tips for Older Adults": www.helpguide.org/articles/sleep/how-to-sleep-well-as-you-age.htm

Hydration for Health: www.h4hinitiative.com

National Center for Complementary and Integrative Health: www.nccih.nih.gov/health/aging

National Council on Aging, "Senior Hunger and Nutrition": www.ncoa.org/healthy-aging/hunger-and-nutrition/

National Institute on Aging, "Healthy Eating": www.nia.nih.gov/health/healthy-eating

National Sleep Foundation: www.sleepfoundation.org

2.3 FINANCES AND FUTURE PLANNING

"Do we have enough money to get there?"

We are living in a time where all markers point to longer lives—on average—for everyone. And we are able to enjoy this increased longevity because our quality of life has also improved. Living longer and healthier lives has so many upsides, including spending more time with family and friends, pursuing personal interests, and also contributing to our communities longer.

But increased longevity also presents us with unique economic challenges. While life expectancy has increased, medical and other basic costs of living have also continued to rise. Many of us will not have the traditional three-legged retirement stool of Social Security, company pension, and personal savings to rely on for life-long income. Instead, most of us will have contributory plans (a 401k or 403b) and personal savings along with Social Security. These sources of income may or may not be enough to sustain us through retirement.

Finally, we know that many older Americans are not able to adequately prepare for their retirement and later discover they need to cut back on necessities or continue working because otherwise they can't maintain their standard of living. Several studies, including one by the U.S. Government Accountability Office in 2017, indicate many baby boomers are not on track to be able to afford basic expenses in retirement.[28]

And the Employee Benefit Research Institute, an organization that tracks important markers related to retirement, reports that many workers expect to work to age 70 or beyond because they cannot yet afford to retire, are uncertain about government benefits, and several other factors.[29] Use of financial planners or financial planning tools remains low. On the positive side, many workers who are retired and have saved for retirement report general confidence in being able to sustain themselves during retirement.

In short, while we should all celebrate the longevity bonus, we must also prepare carefully for the years ahead. This section will not cover all of the ins and outs of financial planning or retirement planning. Many books and financial tools are available that can help you plan your long-term financial future. Instead, this section aims to help put you in the mindset of reflecting on your personal spending habits and optimizing your financial world in small ways that can have a big impact on helping you achieve your retirement goals. In addition, this chapter will encourage you to incorporate advance care—in a step-by-step manner—into your planning.

YOUR FINANCIAL JOURNEY

Your path to financial fitness is as unique as you are. But there are a few basic elements you will need in order to build a sound financial roadmap: retirement planning and adjustments, money management and budgeting basics, advance care and estate planning, and optimizing your living situation.

We've structured this journey as a trip, so get ready to pack your bags and hit the road.

SET YOUR COMPASS AND PLAN YOUR TRIP

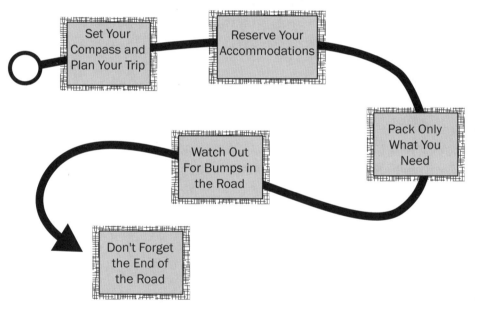

Your financial fitness journey

To get to where you're going, you need to know not only where you are, but what kind of traveler you are. Defining the starting point and direction of your financial journey is just as important as understanding your motivations, goals, and spending habits. Taking the time to calibrate your compass now will help ensure that you're headed in the right direction later.

How do you calibrate your financial compass? First, you need to fully assess your financial situation. Start by gathering information: If your financial information is not already organized and easy to access, bring this information together. You can find free financial assessment forms online or in financial planning workbooks at the bookstore.

Once you have your financial information in hand, determine how much you have on hand in terms of cash, liquid assets (which you can easily convert to cash), and illiquid assets (which cannot be cashed in quickly). Also, list your debts or liabilities such as how much you owe to others in terms of loans, credit cards, lines of credit, and so forth. And finally, understand your cash flow situation: How much money is coming in (income) and going out (expenses) on a monthly basis? Is your cash flow steady or does it vary wildly over time? Is your net cash flow positive or negative? Are you gradually saving or losing money?

If you already use financial software to help organize your financial life and track your cash flow, you're one big step ahead in this process. If you don't currently use a financial software tool or app, you might consider using one. These tools can help take the guesswork out of budgeting and also give you a one-stop-shopping location for all of your accounts.

TIPS

Give your finances a tune up with EconomicCheckUp®, NCOA's free website with a number of useful tools to help you manage your money and revisit your financial goals regularly: www.EconomicCheckUp.org.

Only when you get your bearings can you begin to plan your trip. In which direction will you set out? Where do you want to be in a month, in six months, in a year, in five years? And so on. Do this with an open mind and the knowledge that you will likely need to adjust your goals as time passes. Couple your short-term and long-term goals with strategies for reaching them. Jot them down in a simple table format with "Goals" in one column and "Strategies" in the second column. Once you have a general list of your financial goals, you might want to seek advice from trusted publications and financial advisers. Many community-based organizations offer free or low-cost financial workshops and sometimes offer the option of meeting with a certified financial planner.

TIPS

Don't leave money on the table. Do a benefits screening on NCOA's BenefitsCheckUp® (www.BenefitsCheckUp.org), a confidential and free tool that helps you find federal, state, local, and private benefit programs that could help you pay for daily expenses like food, rent, and medicine.

Setting your financial journey goals is empowering. However, if you don't understand **what kind of traveler you are**, you might not reach your desired destinations. Think of this as your financial personality, a personality that has helped guide both your saving and your spending habits throughout your life. You can both acknowledge your financial personality type while also becoming "mindful" and creating positive financial habits that offset habits that may hamper your ability to reach your goals. You can use the spending diary to get a better sense of your spending habits. Try the spending diary for one week.

Write down everything you spend money on—from your morning coffee to your electric bill—in order to become more aware of your spending and more intentional about how you spend going forward.

RESERVE YOUR ACCOMMODATIONS

Your living situation plays a central role in your overall financial journey. Like many, you probably want to stay in your current living space as long as you can. If you own your home—and 80% of older adults do—then your home is very likely your biggest asset. It can also become a weighty liability when costs for home repairs, modifications, and everyday maintenance start to add up. For many people, these extra costs are a real burden. The good news is that you have numerous options for making the most of your living situation, from downsizing to tapping the stored equity of your home (reverse mortgage) to home sharing. You may also be able to receive services and support in your home or community to age in place.

If you decide to move to a smaller home or a more affordable area, you'll want to ask yourself the same questions for your future home. It's also important to take into account that any move can have repercussions with your family. For example, grown children may still feel an attachment to the home they grew up in. They might feel sad or even angry at the idea that the house will be sold and no longer available to them. Sometimes, the prospect of a move just makes it clear to family members that you are aging, and that can be upsetting in itself.

You can't prevent these kinds of reactions, but thinking through them ahead of time may help you prepare. On the other hand, sometimes the downsizing comes at the urging of family members who may be concerned about your ability to take care of the house, your safety, or your financial situation. If someone else is pushing you to make this move, how do you feel about that? Are there things you need to say to them?

Keep in mind that it's your journey, not theirs.

Continuing to live in your current home is another viable option, and tapping into your home's stored value—or equity—can help pay for house upkeep and other expenses over the years. Home equity is the difference between the appraised value of your home and what you owe on any mortgages. A reverse mortgage can allow you to convert some of that home equity into cash.

Reverse mortgages are loans designed specifically for homeowners age 62 and older. They are called reverse mortgages because the lender pays the homeowner instead of the other way around. The money you receive can be used for any purpose. Unlike conventional mortgages, you do not need to make monthly payments on a reverse mortgage for as long as at least one borrower continues to live in the home. However, you do need to keep paying taxes, insurance, and upkeep on the house.

During the time you have the reverse mortgage, the lender charges interest and adds it to the amount you borrowed instead of making you pay it monthly. This means that the amount you owe gets bigger and bigger, the longer you have the loan. This can use up your equity over time. When the last borrower moves out of the home or dies, the loan becomes due in full, including the amount you borrowed and the interest that was added, as well as interest on the interest. The loan is usually repaid by the borrower or their heirs through selling the home.

Reverse mortgages are not the right choice for everyone. The decision to tap into your home equity may trigger different emotions. You worked hard to pay off or pay down your mortgage, and the prospect of seeing the loan grow again may be difficult. It may also be important to you to leave an inheritance for your children. You will need to balance your desire to preserve home equity with the risk of not having enough funds to continue to stay at home. Organizations such as GreenPath Financial Wellness (www.greenpath.com or 800-550-1961) provide reverse mortgage counseling services and can walk you through the pros and cons of making this decision.

Another option for financing your living situation is to consider room/house sharing. For example, you might want to rent out a spare bedroom or even share your entire home with someone else. The home sharing economy has blossomed in recent years and there are multiple sites that allow you to rent out part or all of your home for both short and long-term periods.

You might also think about living with your children or other family members. There can be many benefits to such an arrangement for you and for your extended family. Being close to youngsters can be energizing and can encourage you to remain active. You'll want, of course, to think carefully not only about overall family dynamics, but also about practical needs such as home safety and social needs such as moving away from good friends and neighbors.

The journey to a new living situation can present many bumps in the road that you will need to overcome. Sometimes the road looks so rocky that you may postpone making decisions long after you know it's really time to do it. What are the challenges that you are facing? Are you concerned that you won't be able to find a place you like? Are you worried about how your children or other family members will react? Are you dreading the process of sorting out your belongings and deciding what to keep—and what to give away/donate/throw out? When you think about preparing to downsize or refinance, do you feel overwhelmed by the prospect? Do you feel sad when you think of leaving your familiar place and starting over?

This can be a long and winding road with several planned or unplanned detours, or a highway leading to a single destination. You may make multiple moves in your lifetime—from a large family home to a smaller one, to an apartment, to a retirement community, then to a care facility or the home of a family member. Each kind of move has its own set of challenges.

To balance out your worries about changing your living situation, think about what you are looking forward to at the end of this journey. What bright horizons are beckoning you? What are you hoping for? Relief from financial strain? Greater safety and security? New social opportunities? More time with your family? New places to see and explore? A new home to decorate and make your own? If you could leapfrog over all the challenges, what benefits would you be enjoying?

If you are feeling very sad, angry, or afraid about the prospect of changing your living situation to the point where you can't find anything positive to look forward to, you may not be ready for this step yet. Consider seeking help from a friend, trusted advisor, or mental health professional who can help you express and deal with your concerns.

AMPlify Your Behavior

Create as vivid a picture as you can of the good things you hope to find in your living situation whether you decide to stay in your home or move. Holding on to this picture can help sustain you through some of the hard parts of making a change. Write a description focusing on the positives.

PACK ONLY WHAT YOU NEED

Possessions. The word itself sounds daunting. And, over the years, our possessions can become daunting presences in our lives. Whether you decide to move or you decide to stay in your own home, you'll want to begin the process of letting go of some possessions. The prospect of choosing what to keep and what to let go of can seem overwhelming, but if you take a step-by-step approach to de-cluttering and do a little at a time, the overall process will not seem as overwhelming.

A few simple questions should guide you in this part of your journey:

- Do I use this item or enjoy this frequently? When was the last time I used this?
- Do I love this item? Does owning this make me happy?

If you don't use an item at least once a year, and you don't feel sad about not having it in your life, this might be something to let go of. Begin by listing the rooms or spaces that you have (bedroom, kitchen, bathroom, yard, etc.). For each space, make a list of the things you know you will definitely *need* and will use. Next, think about things you definitely *want*. These might be some of the same things on the previous list, but there might be some others, items such as books, decorative objects, and photos that have meaning for you. Physically walk through these spaces to see what jumps out at you as being essential to your life and happiness. You might need to go through this process several times, gradually working your way through your home.

Trimming your possessions can be a very difficult process. Or maybe you'll feel relief at the lightening of your load. Most people feel some of both, with worry at the beginning and a surprising amount of relief as they progress. Remember that letting go of items does not mean that others may not make use of them. In fact, this kind of contribution can be extremely satisfying and rewarding. It's a win-win when you can give furniture and kitchen items to a younger family member for their first apartment. Or maybe a neighbor would like some of your garden tools that you no longer use.

Numerous local and national charities take donations, and you can also give directly to someone via sites (such as Freecycle.org) that operate in several localities. You choose someone to give your item to and make arrangements for them to pick it up. Because you are giving to a specific person, this can be almost as satisfying as giving to someone you know.

AMPlify Your Behavior

De-cluttering your life should extend beyond physical items. Do some quick financial de-cluttering on a regular basis to keep your financial life in order:

- Reconcile your bank statement(s) each month
- Check credit card statement(s) closely
- Set up automatic bill payment for fixed expenses
- Use direct deposit for paychecks, tax refunds, benefits payments, etc.
- Shred documents with personal/financial information before disposing of or recycling them

WATCH OUT FOR BUMPS IN THE ROAD

No journey ever goes entirely as planned. Obstacles can set themselves before us and block our way, at least temporarily. Some of these obstacles are all but impossible to fully predict. For example, an unforeseen illness or injury can land us in the hospital with medical expenses that we had not anticipated. However, even though a particular medical event might be unpredictable, incurring medical costs after the age of 65 is well documented. In fact, Fidelity Benefits Consulting estimates that couples should expect an average of $275,000 in health care expenses after age 65.[30] Setting aside funds in your retirement planning for medical expenses is crucial.

Another obstacle that disproportionately impacts older adults is the financial scam. Older adults are thought to have a significant amount of money sitting in their bank accounts, making them attractive to con artists. Millions of older adults, both wealthy and low-income, become victims of fraud every year. Family members, friends, and caregivers have also been known to exploit vulnerable seniors. In your financial and advance care planning, you should take precautions to prevent potential exploitation by appointing a trusted financial power of attorney and health care proxy long before you might need their services.

TIPS

Here are eight ways to protect yourself from scams:

1. Be aware that you are at risk from strangers—and from people close to you.

2. Do not isolate yourself—stay involved with friends, family, and community activities.

3. Always tell salespeople: "I never buy from (or give money to) anyone who calls or visits me unannounced. Please send me your information in writing."

4. Shred all receipts with your credit card number.

5. Sign up for the Do Not Call Registry (www.donotcall.gov) to prevent telemarketers from calling and to take your name off multiple mailing lists. Phone: 1-888-382-1222.

6. Use direct deposit for benefit checks to prevent checks from being stolen from the mailbox.

7. Never give your credit card, banking, Social Security, Medicare, or personal information over the phone unless you initiated the call.

8. Be skeptical of all unrequested offers and thoroughly do your research if you are seeking any type of services. Also, be sure to get references when possible.

NCOA has additional money management tips and scam prevention information at www.ncoa.org/economic-security.

One obstacle that we'll touch on is **financial interdependency**. Have you become "the family bank"? More likely than not, at one time in your life, you have provided financial support to one or more members of your family. (You may have also provided financial support to friends.) Making large loans over the years to family members can contribute to not having enough left for retirement or not being able to stretch your retirement savings long enough. Without a written contract, such loans may be considered gifts that do not need to be repaid. In the worst cases, family financial interdependency can be a big drain on your nest egg and can even push you into poverty.

This doesn't mean you should never help a family member in distress. It does mean you should review your situation carefully to avoid being exploited and to establish whether you can loan or gift funds and still stay on track financially. Establishing boundaries and contracts will help you avoid feeling stressed or overburdened if you choose to give a financial gift. Also, carefully consider your own financial personality when it comes to giving. And, if your generous personality is working against you, you need to take steps to protect yourself. No matter how much you want to help out, remember that family financial interdependencies can have a big impact on your retirement savings.

DON'T FORGET THE END OF THE ROAD

It's not something we like to think about, but it's a reality of life: Our life's journey will end one day. And along that part of the journey, we may also encounter serious illness—one time or more than once. In addition to the direct impact on your health, serious illness often means that others might need to make health care and financial decisions on your behalf.

On this part of the road, advance care planning will help ensure that your wishes, rights, and finances are preserved in times of health incapacity.

In much of this playbook, we've encouraged you to chart your own journey through the dimensions of aging. In the case of advance care planning, we're going to be a little more prescriptive and put forth a recommended path for you.

And, as with all things Aging Mastery®, it involves a series of steps.

Eight Steps to Advance Care Planning

Advance care planning should always be thought of as a process with the following eight steps:

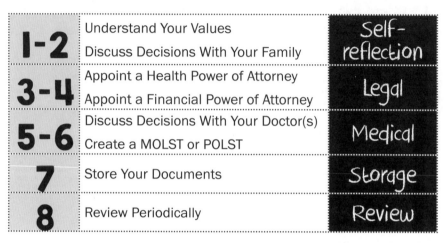

1-2	Understand Your Values Discuss Decisions With Your Family	Self-reflection
3-4	Appoint a Health Power of Attorney Appoint a Financial Power of Attorney	Legal
5-6	Discuss Decisions With Your Doctor(s) Create a MOLST or POLST	Medical
7	Store Your Documents	Storage
8	Review Periodically	Review

Eight steps to creating an actionable advance directive

It is helpful to think of these steps as five distinct types of actions:

- **Self-reflection** and meaningful conversations with family and loved ones about your end-of-life care wishes before serious illness occurs.

- **Legal** actions to appoint health power of attorney and financial power of attorney.

- **Medical** conversations and actions to create a MOLST or POLST.

- **Storage** to ensure timely access to needed information and documentation.

- **Periodic review** to ensure that documents reflect current wishes and circumstances.

Self-reflection

Thinking about your values and beliefs is the necessary—if sometimes difficult and uncomfortable—first step in advance planning. As humans, we are remarkably well equipped to handle adversity, overcome limitations, and adapt to new realities. At the same time, we all have a vision of what our life can and should look like, what gives meaning to us, and what we enjoy doing. Illness, however, can bring unwelcome and unexpected clouds to that clear vision and present obstacles that are no longer easy to overcome.

Writing down your wishes for end-of-life care will help you better understand the types of medical situations that require decisions. It will also empower you to be the key person who makes those decisions.

Take your time with this step. Be prepared to confront some difficult questions such as:

- How long would I want to continue medical treatment in the face of a terminal illness?

- How long would I want to continue treatment in the face of dementia?

- Am I willing to lose a critical ability (to walk, speak, eat, etc.) and continue living?

- When would I want to begin palliative care?

- Would I want to donate my organs?

- Do I need to have all family members in agreement with my decisions?

- How do my spiritual beliefs play a part in my decisions?

TIPS

Five Wishes (www.agingwithdignity.org) and PREPARE for Your Care™ (www.prepareforyourcare.org) offer guided exercises and prompts to walk you through the advance planning process. Five Wishes is available in both print and online formats, and there is a small cost for it. The resulting document that you create meets the legal requirements for an advance directive in 42 states. PREPARE for Your Care™ is an online tool and is free.

If you would like to attend a class on this topic, see if your local community center or health network offers Respecting Choices® or Caring Conversations®.

Your own experiences will likely play a part in your own comfort level with medical treatment and care. You may have a good idea of what type of care you would want or not want based on your experience seeing family members confront a difficult illness.

Once you have reflected on your values and wishes, and written these down, the next step is to have "the conversation" with your family. Talk with your loved ones about your wishes. Tell them where you keep your advance care planning documents and give them a copy if you feel comfortable. While it may be difficult to discuss this with your friends and family, everyone benefits from knowing your wishes. For tips on how to have this conversation—and for inspirational stories—visit The Conversation Project's website (www.theconversationproject.org).

Legal and Medical Actions

The next steps in your advance planning process involve appointing a health care proxy, filling out a medical power of attorney form, assigning a power of attorney for financial matters, and speaking with your health care team.

Naming a proxy (or proxies) is perhaps the most important task you can undertake as part of planning your advance directives. You will be trusting this person, quite literally, with your life. Your proxy might be a family member, a friend, your lawyer, or someone with whom you worship. You will want to have a proxy who:

- Shares your views and values about life and medical decisions.

- Meets the legal criteria in your state for acting as agent or proxy or representative.

- Lives near enough to be able to act on a moment's notice.

- Will be a strong advocate for you and can handle conflicts among family members or with medical staff.

Usually it is best to name one person or agent to serve at a time, with at least one successor, or back-up person, in case the first person is not available when needed. You can also decide how much authority your proxy has over your medical care. Make sure they are comfortable with this responsibility. Once you have decided upon a proxy, complete a medical power of attorney form to officially appoint this person. You can also include instructions for decision-making in this document.

In addition to thinking about your medical care preferences, you'll want to ensure that your financial documentation is in order and that you have completed a will that makes both your financial and burial wishes known. Consider choosing a trusted financial agent. This person may or may not be the same as your health care proxy. Factors to consider in choosing a financial agent include: understanding the pros and cons of power of attorney, learning about joint ownership of bank accounts, and thinking through representative payee and other tools for financial management.

Another step in the legal and medical process is to actually meet with your doctor and discuss your wishes after giving him/her a copy of your advance care planning document for the medical record. Make sure a copy of the document is in your medical record and that your doctor understands and is willing to follow your wishes. You may also want to complete some additional forms known as POLST (Physician Orders for Life-Sustaining Treatment) and MOLST (Medical Orders for Life-Sustaining Treatment). These forms provide more detailed guidance about your medical care preferences and medical interventions such as intubation, antibiotic use, and feeding tubes. Once signed by your doctor, they have the force of any other medical order. Not every state uses these forms, so check with your state department of health to see if they are applicable in your state.

Storage and Periodic Review

On a practical level, advance planning really is just about that— planning. However, on a more fundamental level, advance planning is truly a gift to yourself and your loved ones.

Because it is a gift, you'll want to store all documents related to advance planning carefully and in a location where you and your proxy can easily find them. Plan on making several copies.

Your thoughts about end-of-life care will likely change over the years based on your personal experiences and continued reflection on your life. Revisiting your advance planning decisions on a continual (even annual) basis is as important as making the decisions in the first place. According to the American Bar Association, you should review your documents when any of the following five D's occur:

- You reach a new **DECADE**.

- You experience a **DEATH** in the family or of a friend.

- You **DIVORCE**.

- You receive a new **DIAGNOSIS**.

- You have a significant **DECLINE** in your condition.

WRAP-UP: YOUR AMP FINANCES AND FUTURE PLANNING GUIDEPOSTS

 Use the following guideposts to encourage optimal behaviors related to your finances and future planning. If you are already doing these activities, super! If you are not doing these activities, think about ways that you can set goals and change your behaviors. Remember that the guideposts are markers for your Aging Mastery® journey. Your personal situation and abilities will impact how you incorporate these activities into your life.

Finances and Future Planning Guideposts

	How often?
I have a spending budget and keep to it.	Daily
I am on the alert for financial scams.	Daily
I do what I can to increase my income or reduce my expenses.	Weekly
I keep important financial and personal records in order.	Monthly
I review my Medicare and other insurance plans for both coverage and costs.	Yearly
I assess my living situation and consider rightsizing options.	Yearly
I have an advance care plan and keep it updated, and talk to my family about my end-of-life choices.	Yearly
I meet with a financial planner and benefits advisor to review both my current and long-term needs.	Yearly

SELECTED RESOURCES: FINANCES AND FUTURE PLANNING
Book
Marie Kondo: *The Life-Changing Magic of Tidying Up: The Japanese Art of Decluttering and Organizing*

Websites and Other Media
AARP Foundation ElderWatch: www.aarp.org/aarp-foundation/our-work/income/elderwatch/

American Bar Association, Commission on Law and Aging, "Health Care Decision-Making": www.americanbar.org/groups/law_aging/resources/health_care_decision_making.html

BenefitsCheckUp®: www.BenefitsCheckUp.org

The Conversation Project: www.theconversationproject.org

EconomicCheckUp®: www.EconomicCheckUp.org

Eldercare Locator: www.eldercare.gov

Money Smart for Older Adults: www.fdic.gov/consumers/consumer/moneysmart/olderadult.html

National Council on Aging, "Home Equity": www.ncoa.org/economic-security/home-equity/

National Council on Aging, "Money Management": www.ncoa.org/economic-security/money-management

National Institue on Agin, "Advance Care Planning": www.nia.nih.gov/health/caregiving/advance-care-planning

Social Security Administration, "Retirement Planner": www.ssa.gov/planners/retire

2.4 CONNECTIONS AND COMMUNITY

> *"It's your fault, Eeyore. You've never been to see any of us. You just stay here in this one corner of the Forest waiting for the others to come to you. Why don't you go to them sometimes?"*
>
> *Eeyore was silent for a little while, thinking.*
>
> *"There may be something in what you say, Rabbit," he said at last. "I have been neglecting you. I must move about more. I must come and go."*
>
> — *The House at Pooh Corner*, A. A Milne

Who doesn't feel like Eeyore now and then? We all get comfortable in our own settings. We look around us and think, "I have everything I need right here." A favorite chair. The way the furniture is arranged. Photographs. Special mementos and collections. It all brings comfort. The regularity of daily routines is also reassuring and we may intentionally close the door to new experiences so as not to upset these routines or stir up old troubles. It is no wonder that the phrase "set in their ways" usually refers to older adults.

But, like Eeyore, we must all acknowledge that our social connections won't just happen. We cannot expect people to always come to us; we need to move about more and go to them.

Staying socially engaged as you age and maintaining healthy relationships are key aspects of Aging Mastery®. In a very real sense, they are the glue that connects all of the dimensions of aging well. In the same way that we exercise to maintain physical strength and flexibility, we have to work diligently to maintain and create strong relationships. They won't just happen. As we lose close ties through retirement, moving, family issues, illness, and other factors, this effort becomes even more vital.

Take part in the life of your community. Even if you feel more comfortable being alone most of the time, social isolation will put you at risk and leave you vulnerable to health problems and emotional issues. Healthy social connections positively impact your physical health, your emotional well-being, and your mental faculties. To take the greatest advantage of your longevity, you need to be actively engaged. Most important, you can live a richer, healthier, more fulfilling life by getting out of your corner of the forest to create more and better connections with loved ones, family members, friends, and neighbors in your community.

CONNECTIONS ARE CRITICAL

Social connections are important throughout life, but their importance takes on added weight as we age and our life circumstances change.

Friends, colleagues, and neighbors can bring us laughter, companionship, advice, and comfort. With our closest allies, we share our good times as well as our difficult times, and we return the companionship that they give us. This exchange helps give us meaning in our own lives. Building self-worth, by itself, would be a good enough reason to have lasting relationships. But increasingly people are realizing the health benefits of having strong social connections, and friends can play a role in relieving stress and helping us fight or recover from illness. Having and maintaining strong relationships is truly worth the investment.

Risks of Isolation and Loneliness

Research consistently shows that feeling connected and involved benefits both mental and physical health. But there is a perilous flip side to this coin: In the same way that strong social connections can help us maintain health, isolation has been linked to higher rates of mortality from breast cancer, high blood pressure, heart disease, and other chronic illnesses. Other sobering data[31-32] links isolation to dementia, increased risk of falls, and a higher likelihood of engaging in unhealthy behaviors. In fact, researchers believe that isolation can be just as detrimental to health[33] as smoking and is worse than being obese.

It's estimated that 1 in 5 older adults over the age of 65 lives alone. These individuals can face physical, cultural, and/or geographical barriers that isolate them from their peers and communities. A domino effect often occurs. Limited transportation options cause missed medical appointments or exercise classes, thus potentially making a bad health condition even worse. Isolation also opens individuals to scams and exploitation at higher rates, thus also impacting economic security and the ability to live independently.

The evidence is clear: Making and maintaining connections is vitally important to both your health and economic well-being. These connections don't necessarily come about automatically. And, as you age, you will see many connections slip away or disappear entirely. To keep connections going will take a hefty amount of work, a tablespoon of mindfulness, and a pinch of open-mindedness and willingness to explore new connections.

The Winding Road of Adult Friendships

Think about how you made friends when you were younger. Maybe you had a group of friends or a best friend in your neighborhood, at school, on a sports team, in a music group, or in a club. There were many opportunities to make social connections and see these people on a daily basis.

As an adult, your life has evolved, and it may have become more difficult to make and maintain connections. The responsibilities that come with being an adult can sometimes mean that daily social connections take a back seat. Our circumstances change, and friends can come in and out of our lives.

Most of you will identify with one or more of the following changes and challenges related to your social connections:

Change	Challenge
You've retired or changed your job.	You no longer see colleagues daily.
You've recently moved.	You feel that you have to "start from scratch."
You've moved several times in your life.	Your circle of friends is not constant and you find it difficult to keep in touch with friends in multiple locations.
You've recently divorced or ended a long-term relationship.	You've lost mutual connections and/or feel intimidated by the prospect of dating again.
Your friends have died or moved away.	You're saddened by this, and maintaining a social network has become difficult.
You've lost mobility.	You simply can't get out as much as you used to, if at all.
You care for someone who is ill.	You spend most of your free time running errands or going to medical appointments.

These changes can be gradual. Taken individually, they might not seem significant. For example, retirement may mean that you no longer see your colleagues daily, but you might see friends and family more often so the impact of loss is not felt immediately. Over time, though, the cumulative effect of these changes can have a lasting impact on your social connections.

Our living situations can also limit our connections to others. As we age, the likelihood of living alone—either for short or long periods—increases. Additionally, more and more of us either do not have children who live nearby or do not have children at all, and that means fewer family members to provide company and care. While living alone does not inevitably lead to social isolation, it is certainly a predisposing factor to keep in mind.

With some of the challenges of making and maintaining connections, it's easy to see why we risk becoming isolated as we get older and how easy it can be to fall into this situation. These challenges, though, are exactly the reason why it's so important to keep in touch with friends and with family, and to stay engaged in activities that interest you.

AMPlify Your Behavior

Many other people face the same challenges that you face in remaining connected to others or in forming new friendships. Understanding that it might take time to build a friendship or that you may have to seek out friends via new avenues is a first step to getting out of your corner of the forest. Here are a few options for social engagement.

- Volunteer. (If transportation is a hurdle, consider virtual volunteering.)
- Sign up for a class at your senior center, community college, or a lifelong learning institute.
- Join a group or start a new group of your own such as a walking group or book club.
- Take a trip with Road Scholar, an educational travel organization for adults.
- Attend community events to meet people with similar interests.
- Take on a part-time job.
- Invite a neighbor or acquaintance to spend time and get to know each other.

BUILDING HEALTHY RELATIONSHIPS

Connections are critical for our mental, physical, and emotional well-being, as we've seen. But connections alone will not guarantee well-being: The connections need to be healthy ones. How you form and nurture relationships that are as healthy and strong as they can be is equally important to forming the relationships in the first place.

All relationships are not created equal. No two are alike, and each is the product of experience. Adult relationships can easily be impacted by the ways in which we bonded with adults and peers when we were younger. These lifelong behaviors can serve us well particularly if we have always been able to create strong and healthy relationships. However, if our habits have led us to create less-than-healthy relationships over many years, those same habits will follow us into old age. In order to keep a strong circle of support, it's time to change those habits that do not serve you well.

Create a Relationship "Bill of Rights"

Even the best relationships benefit from guardrails. Setting boundaries and being assertive when necessary are important aspects of long-term relationships. Start by visualizing a healthy, respectful relationship and vocalizing your needs (whether internally or externally). Both are essential to creating lasting friendships that promote your well-being and do not drag you down. Which aspects of your relationships bring you joy? Which give you pause? Write these down then create a "law" for each one to keep you on equal footing in your relationships. The example bill of rights below can help get you started.

I have the right to—
- Be happy in my relationships.
- Have and express my own feelings and opinions, whether or not others agree.
- Express my emotions in a healthy, constructive, and non-threatening manner.
- Be an equal when making decisions.
- Choose my own friends and maintain those relationships.
- Be understood and cared for.
- Live free from fear and abuse.
- End a relationship if it's not healthy for me.

As you seek to form and improve your social connections, you will also want to protect yourself from relationships that are unhealthy. This may first require the ability to recognize if you are currently in such a relationship or if one is forming. There are many places to get help in recognizing and handling a relationship that is not in your best interest, whether it is simply annoying or abusive and dangerous. Most communities have support groups or social services that can help.

Refresh Your Communications Skills

Relationships—even ones that have gone sour—can improve through practicing healthy communication strategies. These strategies are not only useful for building your relationships with friends, family members, and co-workers, they can also help you do a better job of obtaining information from—or giving information to—doctors and other health care workers, professionals such as lawyers and accountants, and customer service staff.

Recognizing that communication barriers can surface at any time is the first step to heading them off before they happen—or at least limiting their harmful effects. The second step is to communicate with purpose.

AMPlify Your Behavior

Here are some communications strategies to help you clarify intentions, reduce the likelihood of misunderstandings, and create a safe space for conversation. We call these the four L's:

- **Listen**. Listen actively to confirm that you hear another's concerns.
- **Learn**. Understand their perspective to target your responses to their needs.
- **Lean in**. Be assertive, set healthy boundaries while still respecting the needs of others, and negotiate to create a "win-win."
- **Love**. Empathize to put yourself in the other person's shoes and acknowledge feelings to create a bond of mutual understanding.

Challenge yourself: How can you incorporate the four L's into your conversations this week?

Employing sound communication strategies can help defuse many conflicts and even salvage frayed relationships. Is there a particular relationship that you wish to improve? Is it time to bury the hatchet of an old grievance? Reaching out to old friends, past acquaintances, and estranged family members to re-initiate relationships that have languished over time can be empowering. Having tough and open conversations may help you see situations from a new perspective. Just remember to be judicious as you approach old territory and be prepared to practice forgiveness, another powerful communication tool.

CONNECTING TO THE COMMUNITY

You are a citizen of the world. In addition to growing and nurturing your personal connections, you'll also want to spend time attending to your community connections. The two often go hand in hand: Getting more involved in your community can easily have a positive boomerang effect on your personal connections!

In the broadest sense of Aging Mastery®, civic engagement means using your gift of time to help others and contribute to the world at large. From small acts of kindness and connecting across generations to being a caregiver or volunteering for a cause, there are many ways to help others. Ultimately, your involvement can be valuable to others and the community. Focus on doing something that you love and that engages you with other people.

Start Small

It may feel like a daunting task to immerse yourself in a civic activity. Your time or your means of transportation might be limited; you just may not know where to start or what you'd like to do. Take a deep breath and look around: The opportunity for civic engagement is right in front of you in the form of a small act of kindness.

An act of kindness is a spontaneous gesture of goodwill toward someone or something: our fellow humans, the animal kingdom, nature. When we are more intentional about being kind to others, we help them and ourselves.

Scientific and behavioral studies increasingly show what many of us know instinctively: Kindness begets kindness. Cooperative behavior not only makes us feel good as individuals, it may also be an element that enables our survival. The more that we cooperate and show generosity, the more others around us become cooperative and generous.

As humans, we form bonds with many different people in our lives. Some bonds are long-lasting such as our bonds with relatives and friends. Other bonds are shorter lasting but can still provide positive well-being benefits. Everything we do has an impact of some kind, and our small acts of kindness can have the greatest ripple effects.

Grow Your Impact

Take the energy and positive feelings that you get from small acts of kindness and put it to service on a larger scale. Civic engagement is a term for the ways in which citizens participate in the life of a community in order to improve conditions for others, help shape the community's future, or leave a legacy of positive change. As part of the largest, healthiest, and best educated population of American adults, we have a unique opportunity to contribute in meaningful ways to impact social change and strengthen our communities through civic engagement.

Let your talents, skills, and interests be the driving force in forging your civic engagement. More likely than not, you can match your talents to a cause whether that talent is clerical work, political activism, public speaking, home repair, teaching, or a host of other talents. The list of talents is endless and the needs are many.

Where you live or your mobility can limit your options for civic engagement. But they don't have to. Though volunteering or activism often occurs at organizational sites, many projects can be done from where you live, preferably with others who can help with the project. You can visit with project team members at a group member's residence or at another agreed-upon location such as a public library, community center, or senior center. There are also numerous ways that you can volunteer your time and talents online or over the phone doing activities such as outreach, teaching, or mentorship.

Don't let where you live be a barrier to doing what you love.

AMPlify Your Thinking

Civic engagement makes us feel great, right? Yes—except when it doesn't.

Be honest. Have you ever felt that your time was not valued properly? Have you ever felt that your volunteer work or civic activism was beginning to feel like a job—or worse, a chore? If these feelings are threatening to limit your participation in a cause that you truly love, then it's time to flex your healthy relationship muscles. Establish clear boundaries with the organization and communicate both your concerns and needs. Resolving your concerns will produce the best outcome for you and others.

Civic engagement is demonstrated by a personal ethic to cultivate service, foster engagement in community, and leave a positive legacy. Staying involved in civic life has positive impacts on your health and well-being, too. Also, many who take part in civic engagement find that they get training in a new skill set. Civic engagement may even open the door for you to explore a meaningful second career.

Bridge the Generation Gap

One way you can give back to your community and strengthen your social connectedness with the next generation is through building these bridges between generations. As an older adult, you can share your life experience with younger generations, including lessons learned and your enthusiasm for living life to its fullest now. You can be a mentor, a teacher, a grandparent, an uncle or aunt, or a friend. Mobilizing the experience, wisdom, and fresh perspectives of all ages can improve lives and strengthen communities.

As older adults, we also benefit from these intergenerational relationships. Benefits include companionship, increased exposure to the latest technologies, warm feelings about rendering service, and having a more meaningful life, among many other positive results. In fact, older adults who participate in intergenerational programs report:

- Enhanced life satisfaction.
- Decreased isolation and reduced depression.
- Lower disability and greater well-being.
- Increased brain activity.
- Expanded learning and skills.

You can forge intergenerational relationships through many types of activities. For example, you can get involved in extended family activities, including reunions, storytelling, and family history research with children, grandchildren, and other family members younger than you.

Intergenerational connections can also be found in the form of volunteer activities such as reading to children at the local library, tutoring children and teens in school subjects, or passing along your career wisdom to young adults just getting started in your trade or profession. In addition, oral history projects can enable older adults who are Veterans, or who were adventurers, athletes, professionals, tradesmen, farmers, and more, to share their life experiences with younger generations and have them recorded for posterity.

At this time in your life, you have much to contribute. You can educate people across generations to break down the stereotypes of aging and build bridges. You can engage with people from a different generation in meaningful ways—through public service projects, conversation, work tasks, extended family interactions, and other types of volunteering. Working together across generations will make for stronger communities.

A CAUTIONARY NOTE ON LOSS

We'll end this section with a cautionary note. Yes, research overwhelmingly links our overall well-being to our ability to remain connected socially. However, there is one circumstance—and it's an extremely important one—where the jury is still out on the benefits of strong social connections. You have probably heard about the "widowhood effect," or more colloquially, "dying of a broken heart." Research around this phenomenon shows an increase in the probability of dying soon after a spouse or partner has died. The effect is most pronounced in the first three months after a spouse or partner has died. In this window, the surviving spouse has a 66% increased chance of dying.[34]

There are many different factors, such as dietary health and mental health, that can either worsen or alleviate this effect. Common sense would tell us that strong social connections should mitigate against this effect. But that does not appear to be the case. To date, no study has definitively shown a direct link between strong social connections and the ability to recover from the death of a spouse, though some have pointed to the possibility that friendships can help during these times of transition.[35] We highlight this not to discourage you from making and maintaining social connections, but to underline what you probably already know: There is no single, proven cure for grief and loss.

WRAP-UP: YOUR AMP CONNECTIONS AND COMMUNITY GUIDEPOSTS

 Use the following guidepost to encourage optimal behaviors related to your connections and community engagement. If you are already doing these activities, super! If you are not doing these activities, think about ways that you can set goals and change your behaviors. Remember that the guideposts are markers for your Aging Mastery® journey. Your personal situation and abilities will impact how you incorporate these activities into your life.

Connections and Community Guideposts

	How often?
I practice small acts of kindness.	3-4 days/ week
I practice the art of communicating: listen, learn, lean in, and love.	Daily
I have meaningful connections with people of other generations.	Weekly
If I am a caregiver, I help myself. If not, I help a caregiver.	Weekly
I spend time with friends and family.	Weekly
I participate in a group (or groups) that align with my interests.	Monthly
I am involved in civic causes and community projects to leave a legacy of positive change in the world.	Monthly
I repair or renew relationships that are neglected or frayed.	Monthly

SELECTED RESOURCES: CONNECTIONS AND COMMUNITY
Books
Marci Alboher: *The Encore Career Handbook: How to Make a Living and a Difference in the Second Half of Life*

Marc Freedman: Encore: *Finding Work that Matters in the Second Half of Life*

Websites and Other Media
Connect2Affect: Connect2Affect.org

CreateTheGood: CreateTheGood.org

Encore: www.encore.org

Experience Corps: www.aarp.org/experience-corps

Generations United: www.gu.org

Grandparents Day: www.grandparentsday.org

SeniorCorps: www.seniorcorps.gov

Volunteer Match: www.VolunteerMatch.org

2.5 CREATIVITY AND LEARNING

> *"From around the age of six, I had the habit of sketching from life. I became an artist, and from fifty on began producing works that won some reputation, but nothing I did before the age of seventy was worthy of attention. At seventy-three, I began to grasp the structures of birds and beasts, insects and fish, and of the way plants grow. If I go on trying, I will surely understand them still better by the time I am eighty-six, so that by ninety I will have penetrated to their essential nature. At one hundred, I may well have a positively divine understanding of them, while at one hundred and thirty, forty, or more I will have reached the stage where every dot and every stroke I paint will be alive."*
>
> — *Katsushika Hokusai*

The Japanese painter Katsushika Hokusai[36] (1760–1849) is perhaps best known to us for his paintings of Mt. Fuji, particularly the painting widely known as *The Great Wave*. You have likely seen this painting with its brilliant blues, massive threatening waves, and claw-like whitecaps. Mount Fuji features in the painting, too, but far in the distance and small in size in comparison to the great wave. It is the most reproduced painting in the world today.

There is so much to learn from and be amazed at in Hokusai's words. Let's start with the fact that he regarded his best paintings as those he produced beginning in his 70s. This is a truly remarkable statement especially considering that he painted his entire life, produced thousands of illustrations for prints and for books, and was widely revered as a painter and an art teacher well before the age of 70. But his self-assessment is in many ways accurate: He reached the pinnacle of his career in his 70s and 80s. He was 71 when he created *The Great Wave* along with several other famous paintings of Mt. Fuji.

It would be inaccurate to call Hokusai a "late bloomer." A "continual bloomer" would be a better description, someone for whom learning and creativity went hand in hand his entire life. He experimented constantly, often going against the prevailing art techniques of the time and drawing inspiration from other countries. (In fact, he was kicked out of at least one art school.)

He also bloomed despite many odds against him. In his 60s, his wife died, he had a series of strokes, and he lost money to a profligate grandson. His daughter, also an artist, left her marriage to come live with him. By all accounts, they lived in relative poverty for the rest of his life. He continued to paint in spite of his life's difficulties.

Let's be inspired by his example as we think of ways to let our own creativity and learning bloom, making creative connections in our daily lives.

"If my dog can take up yoga, I can try my hand at painting."

AGE AND THE CREATIVITY/LEARNING CONUNDRUM

Hokusai painted throughout his life and had his most creative years in the last 20 years of a long life. Not only were these years highly creative and productive, they were also filled with learning, experimentation, and innovation. His later-life works stand out and astonish us still because of his pioneering use of a new paint color of his time: Prussian blue. He was constantly experimenting, and that experimentation left a profound impact on the art world, influencing both illustration techniques and great art movements such as Impressionism.

Hokusai's is not the only example of lifelong creativity and learning. Yet, cultural norms and common misconceptions about aging lead many to think that the window for creativity and learning somehow closes at a certain age. The expression, "You can't teach an old dog new tricks," remains persistent in our culture and is reinforced in certain stories and outlier examples. For years, common thinking for scientists held that creativity peaks in a person's early twenties. Einstein himself said: "A person who has not made his great contribution to science before the age of 30 will never do so." It's an intriguing statement and makes you take notice, but it doesn't necessarily reflect reality.[37]

Time and again, the notion that creative genius only occurs when we are young—even genius specifically related to work in the sciences—has been dispelled. In fact, middle age and later are times of great contribution, creativity, and learning. You likely know individuals who have learned a new language, started to paint, or taken up a musical instrument later in life. Maybe you are one of those individuals! Learning might be different from when you were younger and certain skills may take longer to acquire, but the capacity remains.

LEARNING AS A DAILY PRACTICE

Surround yourself with learning. It's really as simple and straightforward as that. The more you intentionally surround yourself with learning, the more natural it will be to make learning part of your routine.

The good news is that you are probably already engaged—to some extent or another—in lifelong learning. The very act of living and being a part of the world puts you in touch with learning and with learning opportunities. Informal learning happens all the time. You wake up and read, watch, or listen to the news. You go grocery shopping and are presented with new items on the shelves. You take a walk and notice something new in nature or a new building in our neighborhood. You are, literally, surrounded by learning opportunities, so surrounding yourself with learning is nearly automatic. The key is to add some intention, a touch of formality, and maybe even a little bit of critical thinking to these everyday experiences to enhance them.

AMPlify Your Behavior

Make learning part of your daily routine by switching up the way you do things.

If every day you . . .	Today, go one step further
Read the newspaper	Take one news item and read about it in more detail or from different points of view.
Listen to your favorite music	Look up the musician online or at the library, and learn more about their history or upcoming shows.
Take a walk in your neighborhood	Stop by your neighbor's garden and ask about their plants.
Watch TV	Swap out your usual program for something different.

What did you learn today that you could share with others? What other ways can you change up your routine and open yourself to new knowledge?

LEARNING WITH A PURPOSE

In addition to making learning a daily practice, you should also consider learning about topics in a more deliberate manner. Think of it as learning for the long term with the goal of simply expanding your knowledge all the way to becoming an expert in something.

> *"Show up, show up, show up, and after a while the muse shows up, too."*
>
> — *Isabel Allende*

Learning a new language is a great example. You may want to become familiar with a language for a trip you've planned and just need to know some basic expressions. Maybe you have a new relative or friend who speaks another language and you want to become more conversant with that person. In that case, you'll want to spend more time perfecting your language skills. In either case, the avenues for learning are numerous from language learning apps and online classes to more traditional books and tapes or classes at your local community college.

Learning with a purpose means being aware of your own learning style and also more generally of how we learn as adults. How we learn as adults differs fundamentally from how we learned when we were children. As adults, we bring rich life experiences to our learning endeavors as well as an internal motivation to learn. Malcolm Knowles, an American educator, observed these features in adult learners and developed an approach to adult instruction that privileged these features to create a more satisfying learning experience.[38-39]

For Knowles, adult learners are more self-directed because their sense of self is more fully developed. This sense of self encourages them to be active participants in their learning and to bring experiences—both positive and negative ones, successes and failures—to what they learn. The sense of self that we have as adults helps us focus both on the relevancy of what we are learning and the application of it to our daily lives.

This last point brings us back to a key feature of Aging Mastery®: turning learning into action. Learning with a purpose also means finding an application for your learning. It's taking the learning that one next step. Sometimes, the application for your learning will be obvious, and you'll have that goal in mind right from the start. If you've taken a series of cooking classes, your next step will be to incorporate those techniques and dishes into your cooking repertoire. If you've taken an art seminar, the next step might be to visit a local art museum or browse an online museum collection.

Sometimes, though, the exact outcome of or purpose for your learning adventure will not necessarily be clear. You may even become frustrated, thinking that you'll never "do anything" with what you've learned. More often than not, though, there is an application—an unseen purpose—for what you've learned, and this application will present itself to you at some future point. At that point, you will be able to connect the dots. All of us have examples of this happening in our lives. A very well-known example was given by Steve Jobs during a commencement that he gave in 2005. An excerpt of that speech is in the following box.

"Because I had dropped out [from Reed College] and didn't have to take the normal classes, I decided to take a calligraphy class to learn how to do this. ... It was beautiful, historical, artistically subtle in a way that science can't capture, and I found it fascinating. None of this had even a hope of any practical application in my life. But 10 years later, when we were designing the first Macintosh computer, it all came back to me. And we designed it all into the Mac. It was the first computer with beautiful typography. If I had never dropped in on that single course in college, the Mac would have never had multiple typefaces or proportionally spaced fonts. ... Of course it was impossible to connect the dots looking forward when I was in college. But it was very, very clear looking backward 10 years later. Again, you can't connect the dots looking forward; you can only connect them looking backward. So you have to trust that the dots will somehow connect in your future. You have to trust in something—your gut, destiny, life, karma, whatever. This approach has never let me down, and it has made all the difference in my life."

—Steve Jobs, excerpted from his 2005 Stanford University commencement address

How do you connect the dots in your life? Have you ever found that something you learned years ago has a surprising new meaning for you today? Do you enjoy learning for the sake of learning, even if the topic does not seem directly applicable to your life today?

CRACKING OPEN THE DOOR TO CREATIVITY

Becoming creative or doing something creative can seem like a daunting undertaking for many of us or something that we simply have no interest in doing. One stumbling block is an in-built resistance to creativity that is difficult to overcome, especially if we either were never encouraged to be creative or if our early efforts at creativity were thwarted. How many of us reflexively say "I can't draw" or "I can't carry a tune," and then just move on with our daily lives? Another stumbling block is not knowing how or where to begin. We might feel overwhelmed with choices and ideas or, conversely, not have any idea where our creative interests might lie.

If any of these stumbling blocks sound familiar to you, we'd like to offer a couple of doorways that may help you break through these barriers and bring creativity into your life. The first approach involves trying something new for a short period of time; the second approach involves telling your life story in a variety of ways.

"Find something you're passionate about and keep tremendously interested in it."

— Julia Child

Door #1. Try something new for 30 days

In 2011, Matt Cutts spoke for three and a half minutes on a TED stage and urged his audience to "try something new for 30 days."[40] The idea itself, as he said, was not new: What was notable was that he actually followed through on the idea and learned that trying something new for 30 days not only helped him accomplish activities he had always wanted to do, but also gave him the courage and confidence to tackle things he never thought were possible. In order to jumpstart your own experience with creativity, how about trying something new for 30 days? As Matt so eloquently said, "I guarantee you the next 30 days are going to pass whether you like it or not, so why not think about something you have always wanted to try and give it a shot!" We like the directness of this approach and also the fact that it is time-limited. You are not committing to an extended period of time, so the prospect of doing the activity is not overwhelming. At the same time, 30 days will give you at least an idea of whether you are interested in the creative pursuit and want to spend more time with it.

Door #2. Burst open your life story

Experiment with telling your life story in a variety of forms. Imagine your life story in the following forms:

- **Movie**. What kind of movie is your life? Who are the main actors? What's the story line?

- **Haiku or limerick**. How can you condense your life to its most important parts?

- **Song**. What genre of music describes your life? What is the refrain?

- **Recipe**. What are the main ingredients to your life? How do they fit together? What is the resulting dish?

Have fun with this activity. Doing it with family members—especially youngsters—and friends could bring out a creative side you didn't know you had.

Do you have a Door #3 that you already use to explore creativity? How would you approach opening the door to creativity?

ESTABLISH A CREATIVE ROUTINE

The words "creative" and "routine" may not sound like they belong together, but they do. And establishing habits in your creative pursuits is really identical to forming good health habits or sound financial habits. Think of creativity as a muscle that needs to be stretched and strengthened every day.

Creativity can have moments of inspiration and insight that feel like a lightning bolt. More often than not, though, that lightning bolt comes after days or months or even years of attention and dedication to the creative pursuit. If you're already engaged in creative activities, you know this well. For whatever creative activity you like to do, have the tools of the trade close at hand, if possible. For example, if you like to build things in your woodworking shop, have a sketchpad (either paper or electronic) with you always to jot down ideas and drawings for your creations.

> *"The routine is as much a part of the creative process as the lightning bolt of inspiration, maybe more."*
>
> — *Twyla Tharp*

Establish your routine. Earlier we talked about the built-in resistance to creativity. We can thoroughly convince ourselves that creativity is for others and that we are simply not "creative types." We might hold the notion—which many people do—that creativity and talent is innate. We are either born with it or not. We cannot learn it. That kind of thinking is both counterproductive and goes against what we know from artists, writers, and musicians who have achieved greatness. Greatness involves work and putting in the work helps to achieve skills, big and small. Research in this area by behavioral scientists like Angela Duckworth and Anders Ericcson shows that elements such as "grit" and "deliberate practice" are essential to achievements across many fields.[41-42] Talent may give some people a leg up, but hard work truly does pay off in anything that you set your mind to do.

SHARE YOUR LEARNING, SHARE YOUR WORK

Sharing is in our DNA. As humans, we are programmed to share. We live in a sharing world. Some might think that we overshare and or that sharing is more about self-congratulation than anything else. Yet sharing our creativity can provide a powerful bonding experience with those around us. Drawing simple vignettes of your life and sharing these with your family and friends is an example of a gift with wonderful repercussions. Technology also provides us with incredible tools to share our knowledge and creativity with those we know and with people whom we've never met. The possibilities are endless from creating video tutorials on any subject to writing blogs about a specialty topic, from self-publishing a novel to posting images of your woodshop creations online.

AMPlify Your Thinking

Rosa has lived in a suburb of Washington, DC, for 92 years. She started painting when she was 78, found that she had a knack for it, and really enjoyed it, too. Her output of paintings and collages has been prodigious. But what to do with all of this artwork that she's created over the years?

That's where her 86-year-old neighbor, Walter, comes into the picture. Walter is a retired engineer who scours lumber yards for refuse wood and creates beautiful gazebos and furniture with them. By happy coincidence, he also loves making picture frames.

For the past 15 years, the two have joined forces: Walter makes intricate, three-dimensional frames for Rosa's paintings and collages, and Rosa exhibits these works at places of worship and community centers.

Are you a Rosa? Do you have a Walter living next door or down the block? Do you find new uses for found objects? Can you pool your talent with others to create beauty and share it with the world?

WRAP-UP: YOUR AMP CREATIVITY AND LEARNING GUIDEPOSTS

 Use the following guideposts to encourage optimal behaviors related to your creativity and learning. If you are already doing these activities, super! If you are not doing these activities, think about ways that you can set goals and change your behaviors. Remember that the guideposts are markers for your Aging Mastery® journey. Your personal situation and abilities will impact how you incorporate these activities into your life.

Creativity and Learning Guideposts

	How often?
I bring music into my life.	Daily
I incorporate a sense of play into my life.	Daily
I learn about a new topic or refresh my learning.	Weekly
I take up—and keep up—a hobby.	Weekly
I experiment and change the typical way I do things.	Weekly
I question assumptions to spark new thinking.	Weekly
I create (arts, crafts, gardens, food, etc.).	Monthly
I take part in cultural events.	Monthly

SELECTED RESOURCES: CREATIVITY AND LEARNING
Books
Jocelyn K. Glei: *Manage Your Day-to-Day: Build Your Routine, Find Your Focus, and Sharpen Your Creative Mind*

Mark S. Walton: *Boundless Potential: Transform Your Brain, Unleash Your Talents, Reinvent Your Work in Midlife and Beyond*

Websites and Other Media
The Bernard Osher Foundation (and Lifelong Learning Institutes): www.osherfoundation.org

Coursera: www.coursera.org

edX: www.edx.org

Encore Creativity: www.encorecreativity.org

Foundation for Art and Healing: www.artandhealing.org

National Center for Creative Aging: www.creativeaging.org

Road Scholar: www.roadscholar.org

TED: www.ted.com

Vitality Arts: www.arohaartfulaging.org

2.6 LEGACY AND PURPOSE

> *"And you that shall cross from shore to shore years hence are more to me, and more in my meditations, than you might suppose."*
>
> — *Walt Whitman,*
> *"Crossing Brooklyn Ferry"*[43]

In Aging Mastery®, we strive to make the most of our gift of time. That commitment involves taking small steps to change behaviors, improve our lives, and make meaningful connections. Legacy and purpose are an integral part of this commitment to making the most of our gift of time.

For most of us, our purpose in life may have been clearer in our earlier years. Our roles, and the markers for them, are more obvious. In our youth, we learn and prepare for adulthood. As adults, we become citizens of our communities. We have careers, families, and civic activities that help us attach to these communities. As we've gotten older, our purpose can be less clear. Where do we fit in? How do we continue to contribute? We have to define our roles for ourselves.

People who thrive in their later years, have a purpose larger than themselves. It gives them a reason to get up each morning and face the day with passion and intent. Without a clear sense of purpose, it is easy to focus too much on the personal ailments and losses that are also a part of growing older.

In "Crossing Brooklyn Ferry," Walt Whitman takes his readers on a journey through his legacy through the lens his own life, the lives of others around him, and the environment (both natural and man-made) that binds them all together. He understands that he is not the first person to view this stretch of river or to cross it. Nor will he be the last:

> *"The others that are to follow me, the ties between me and them,*
>
> *The certainty of others, the life, love, sight, hearing of others."*

He celebrates the power of the shared experience he has with this continuum of people—those who are standing with him in the moment, those who came before him, and those who will come after him. Likewise, the river he sees will be both the same as and different from the river of the past, the present, and the future. It's a beautiful meditation that celebrates, in a powerful way, the continuous thread of existence that connects us to the past and to the future.

As Whitman reflects on his own life, he makes note of both the moments that have sparkled and those that have glowed a little less brightly. All of these moments, though—the high points and the low—together form the totality of our lives and make us who we are.

In the Aging Mastery® universe, we have identified three main steps to help you both **reflect upon** your purpose and **take actions** that enhance your own legacy:

1. Reflect on your responsibilities and your life's purpose

2. Create the pathway for your life's purpose to flourish

3. Build your legacy via service to others, teaching, and storytelling

GETTING TO PURPOSE

A sense of purpose can help define our learning pursuits, our career path(s), our volunteer passions, and our hobbies, among other things. This sense of purpose is self-driven, but that does not necessarily mean that it remains the same over time or that it isn't influenced by factors that are not completely in our control.

Think about your own life and consider these questions:

- Has your sense of purpose remained constant over time and have you been able to intentionally fulfill that sense of purpose in both your public and personal life?

- Has your sense of purpose changed or evolved over time due to factors such as availability of education, a change in jobs, or a new relationship?

There is no right or wrong answer to either of these questions. And you may not even have a clear "yes" or "no" response to them. For some of us, our sense of purpose and direction is clear from an early age and in everything we do, we strive toward a goal that aligns with that purpose. For others of us, our sense of purpose is not set in stone and maybe is not even apparent to us at all times. An unexpected change—such as a job layoff or relocation—can present us with a sense of purpose or new direction that we had not consciously considered before.

Our purpose can also be partially defined for us, especially when we move from the "cared-for" years and enter the "caring-for" years of our lives. If we care for children, grandchildren, parents, grandparents, or other family members, our sense of purpose is—in part—dictated by their needs.

All of life's transitions provide opportunities to pause, think about our place in the world, and take actions that help us fulfill our talents. The transition to older age is one such important transition—arguably, the most profound transition that we experience. View this time of your life as an incredible bonus. You've been given a gift of years and a multitude of experiences to draw upon as you continue to learn and grow and fulfill your purpose. We can also refer to this purpose as our calling.

The concept of a calling is familiar in many religious and mythical traditions. In the typical scenario, a person is called upon to tackle a challenging situation. The decision to take on the challenge rests with the person alone. It is an active choice: Either grow and respond to the challenge or accept the status quo. This important decision sets the person on a path to fulfill a mission.

> *"A ship in harbor is safe— but that is not what ships are built for."*
>
> *— John Augustus Shedd*

Some may think of the concept of a calling as a nice-to-have, something to contemplate in our free time, but not necessarily important to our lives. But the stories we read and countless real-life examples prove otherwise: Having that central sense of our calling is fundamental to how we face new, exciting missions and also how we adapt to life's losses or challenges. Moreover, it's **our responsibility** to keep our sense of purpose at the forefront. As Viktor Frankl observed:

"Each man is questioned by life; and he can only answer to life by answering for his own life; to life he can only respond by being responsible."

Frankl's own experience in the Holocaust informed this powerful statement. His observations, both from his perspective as a prisoner and as a physician, led him to conclude that a sense of purpose was foundational to a human being's survival. (His book, *Man's Search for Meaning*, explores this idea fully.) Frankl's response to a dismal and horrifying situation is an exemplar for all of us as we face our own challenges in life.

AMPlify Your Thinking

Callings may present themselves in response to a new opportunity or to a challenge. Think about one such occasion in your past. (It could have been a new job or the loss of a job; a birth or the loss of a family member.) How did you respond? How did having a sense of purpose help you respond? Did you find strength in your sense of purpose?

Now think about an opportunity or challenge you face today. What enables you to address it? What obstacles get in the way of you saying, "I'm ready to take this on"?

MAKE A STATEMENT

A necessary and important part of Aging Mastery® is acknowledging our own mortality. It is a fact of life. Accepting mortality also means accepting our limits. This acceptance, in turn, helps shape the path we create for our legacy to thrive. Acceptance does not come willingly or automatically to any of us, but we hope that concentrating—in a determined way—to create a legacy that reflects the bounty and beauty of your life will help you take steps toward that acceptance.

Taking the time to write out a personal mission statement can provide a first step in the process of accepting our mortality. Your personal mission statement answers the question:

How Would I Like to Be Remembered?

In order to answer the question, you might find it helpful to write down your responses to these questions first:

- What am I most passionate about?

- What are the values that I hold dearest?

- What are the things I still want to achieve?

- What personal qualities do I most want to emphasize in myself?

- What is the impact I would like to have?

We encourage you to write your responses over the course of several days. Even if your responses are clear and obvious to you right away, review them one week from today after giving yourself time to reflect. We encourage you to share your responses with others. Your closest friends and family members can help you validate your passions and values, and provide guidance. Also, do not be afraid to surprise them with your vision of what you want to achieve in life. When they say, "I never knew you were so passionate about music," you can respond by saying, "Yes, it's always been a passion. Can you offer any suggestions to help me fulfill this passion and make an impact?"

PUTTING PURPOSE INTO ACTION

Basic physics says that a body at rest needs a catalyst or force to get it moving. Otherwise, it stays at rest forever. When thinking about your purpose, what is the catalyst or force that will ensure that purpose is front and center in your life?

Reflecting on your sense of purpose, as you've done, is a good first step. We gain energy from looking backward and reflecting on our lives. This reflection grounds us: We take stock of our life's highlights and low points. If we can accomplish this without judgment and with the idea of building on our best selves, then we can move forward and leave a strong legacy in the process.

Here are a few steps to keep in mind as you think about how your own sense of purpose can inform your response to life's opportunities and challenges:

1. Take stock of how your life has contributed to your sense of purpose.

2. Be kind to yourself as you look backward to take in the full expanse of your life.

3. Understand that your life involves movement, evolution, and change.

4. Look ahead toward the future (with as little regret as possible).

The last item is especially important. Thinking that you're "too old" or have "missed the boat" to live your purpose will result in stagnation and the inability to move forward. It can be debilitating to focus on the missed opportunities rather than those opportunities ahead of you.

The act of writing down your purpose and sharing your thoughts with a trusted friend is a great step to take if you feel in a rut. In need of inspiration in this process? Think about the many individuals who have proven that it is truly never too late to pursue a passion. Grandma Moses did not have the time or means to pursue her art career until she was in her late 70s. Her amazing contribution to American art would be lost to us all had she decided to regret the years that she could not devote to her painting.

Setting goals is also an important part of the catalyst that propels you forward and gives you your day-to-day momentum. In this playbook, you've learned that setting goals and writing them down is central to both motivation and accomplishment related to physical activity, keeping your financial affairs in order, developing proper sleep habits, and more.

"It is not enough to be busy. So are the ants. The question is: What are we busy about?"

— *Henry David Thoreau*

We believe that everyone should also have goals related to personal aspirations and purpose, as well. You might call it a bucket list with a purpose. Such a list does more than simply give you bragging rights about your accomplishments; this **purposeful bucket list** should be an expression of your life's journey.

Coming up with ideas for a purposeful bucket list is not difficult on the surface. Off the top of your head, you can probably think of some new skills you would like to learn or a hobby you'd like to pursue. What's more challenging—and what is also essential—is spending time thinking through the **why** of your bucket list as much as the what of your list.

One way to give meaning to your bucket list goals is to imagine an impact of the goal in your community or in the world at large. Making a connection between your aspirations and your community does not need to be difficult. It can be as simple as expanding "learn to cook" to "have a dinner party for my neighbors." If you want to learn to knit, consider whether you could knit 20 scarves and donate them to the homeless.

AMPlify Your Thinking

As important as it is to reflect on your purpose and what impact you want to achieve, it's equally important to reflect on those things that do not interest you, that are not meaningful to you, and that do not serve your life's purpose. Think of this as your "anti-bucket list." What would you include in this list? Are there items on this list that you're doing now that you need to stop doing in order to fulfill your purpose in life?

Thinking about the civic and social connections that could result from your bucket list goal can help you give additional meaning to that goal.

REPAIR WHAT IS BROKEN (AS BEST YOU CAN)

The legacy we leave is dependent on many factors. Some factors—hopefully most of them—are in our control, but some are not. In Aging Mastery®, it's our responsibility to repair any damage we have caused in our lives—whether intentional or not. Likewise, it's incumbent on us to reach out to those who may have harmed us and close the loop on difficult events.

The acts of extending apologies and of reaching out for understanding are hugely beneficial both for our emotional well-being and our ability to fulfill our purpose. Relinquishing hurt and regret goes a long way toward concentrating our energy on the future and moving forward with our life's journey. It helps "lighten the load" and gives us the wherewithal to focus on those things that are most meaningful to us and that have the greatest impact on the world.

AMPlify Your Behavior

Let go of the things that no longer contribute to your life such as regrets, commitments, judgments, and resentments. One way to do this is symbolic, but effective: On a small piece of paper, write down one thing that you would like to let go of. Place the paper in a glass of water and watch the ink disappear.

What other methods do you use to let go of those things that do not contribute to your life?

THE ART OF SHARING

Your legacy is an occasion for joy. Share this joy with others.

Legacy is one of those daunting words that can keep us from doing those things that will form our legacies. Try not to let that happen. Taking small steps has served you well in changing behaviors in the other dimensions of Aging Mastery® and can do the same here.

Here's an example: Let's say you've always wanted to write a memoir to document family history. Writing a memoir can be a daunting task for even the most experienced writers. How can you accomplish this project without feeling overwhelmed? A first step might be to make an audio recording highlighting key events in your life. Encourage family members or friends to help out and share in the experience. They can be your audience while you tell your stories and can also share their stories about you. Enlist the help of others to record or otherwise save this memoir. Next, find photos or other memorabilia associated with the stories that you've preserved. In this way, piece by piece and step by step, you're creating your memoir.

Teaching is another wonderful way to cement your legacy and pass on valuable learnings, but we do not always automatically think of ourselves as teachers. Or, we do not think that there are opportunities for us to teach in our communities. But teaching encompasses so many forms of instructions that can take place in informal settings or formal settings. Most of us are teaching, in one way or another, every day. To teach "with purpose," look for opportunities to connect your passion with teaching. If you love to cook, create lasting memories in your kitchen and teach your family your favorite recipes. Treat the kitchen like a classroom while you measure ingredients and explain the personal meaning behind a favorite dish. If you love to cook, but are no longer able to do so easily, you can still pass on recipes and have family members make your favorite dishes for you.

> *"I've learned that people will forget what you said, people will forget what you did, but people will never forget how you made them feel."*
>
> — *Maya Angelou*

Celebrations should be part of how you think about your legacy as well. Make even the smallest accomplishments an opportunity for a festive occasion. When you complete a project—a woodworking or other craft project, for example— invite people over to see it and share in the joy you receive from making something with your hands.

AMPlify Your Thinking

You've been in training all of your life for this moment. All of your learning, experience, and wisdom has led you to where you are now and prepared you for what you can still accomplish. How will you use your time and talent to make the world better?

WRAP-UP: YOUR AMP LEGACY AND PURPOSE GUIDEPOSTS

 Use the following guideposts to encourage optimal behaviors related to your legacy and purpose. If you are already doing these activities, super! If you are not doing these activities, think about ways that you can set goals and change your behaviors. Remember that the guideposts are markers for your Aging Mastery® journey. Your personal situation and abilities will impact how you incorporate these activities into your life.

Legacy and Purpose Guideposts

	How often?
I create pathways for my life's purpose to flourish.	Daily
I apologize when I am in the wrong.	Daily
I share my life story with others.	Daily
I spend time each day in service to others.	Daily
I share my knowledge with others.	Weekly
I have created and act on a purposeful bucket list.	Monthly
I participate in intergenerational activities.	Monthly
I reflect on my responsibilities and my life's purpose.	Monthly

SELECTED RESOURCES: LEGACY AND PURPOSE
Books
Joan Chittister: *The Gift of Years*

Viktor Frankl: *Man's Search for Meaning*

Websites and Other Media
Generations United: www.gu.org

Public Broadcasting Service, "American Family: Make a Family Tree": www.pbs.org/americanfamily/tree

StoryCorps: www.storycorps.org/great-questions

Section III

ACTIVITIES

Congratulations!

You've learned about Aging Mastery® and the six dimensions of aging well. Along the way, you've been given prompts to reflect on various aspects of your life. We hope you have found these useful and have shared these prompts with others. Now, it's time to put these reflections into action and create the Aging Mastery® path that makes sense for you. In this chapter, we provide a few tools to help you get started: a quick self-assessment exercise, tips for incorporating AMP activities into your daily life, and sample activities for each of the six dimensions of aging.

3.1 GETTING STARTED
The First Step Is Taking a Step Back

Before you dive into the activities of this chapter, take a moment to go through a self-assessment. This assessment will help you identify the areas where you need, or want, to spend the most energy. Those will become your focus areas for the next week or month. You can come back to this again and again. In fact, that's a great way to chart your progress!

Six Dimensions of Aging Self-Assessment

Gratitude and Mindfulness

Health and Well-Being

**Finances and
Future Planning**

**Connections
and Community**

Creativity and Learning

Legacy and Purpose

For each of the six dimensions of aging, we have recommended a few general goals or Aging Mastery® Guideposts. **We've compiled the guideposts together at the end of this section**.

As you look at the list, ask yourself:

1. How am I doing in each dimension of aging?
2. Which activities do I naturally gravitate toward? Why?
3. Are there any activities I avoid spending time on? Which ones and why?
4. What prevents me from doing certain activities?

Answering these questions will provide you with a good, mental snapshot of how you're doing with respect to the Aging Mastery® guideposts and should also get you thinking about what you might want to incorporate into your routine.

• •

Most of us will have areas where we feel confident and in control, and others where we don't know where to start. It's natural to find some things easier to do than others. Also, we may have conditions that limit our ability to do every activity in the guideposts lists. Given all that, we still believe that the key to aging well is to make sure we're tending to every dimension over time.

Taking Things Week by Week

Congratulations on making it this far on the Aging Mastery® journey. Now comes the time when you want to put your learning into action. We know that getting started can be difficult: Sometimes, the best laid plans never materialize. When we set difficult and unachievable goals, for example, we often become frustrated and are reluctant to take that first step. Try not to let that happen here! You are taking the first steps in celebrating the gift of longevity. It's not about competing with others, and it's not about perfection.

It's all about making the most of your gift of time in ways that are meaningful to you.

When you're first getting started, it can be helpful to set a weekly intention to help guide your activity choices. From the list of Aging Mastery® Guideposts, start first with the ones that you tend to avoid and make one of these your focus for the first week.

The next part of this section has several suggestions for activities to do in each dimension. These activities are designed to help you reach some of the Aging Mastery® Guideposts. You'll notice that each activity has a suggested time length. To make sure your daily goal is manageable, first pick the shorter activities before tackling the longer ones.

At the end of the week, check in with yourself:

- How do you feel?
- What impact, if any, did the activities have on your overall well-being?
- What did you like? What didn't you like?
- Could you see yourself doing this activity on a more regular basis?

You can keep track of your weekly intentions and activities in a notebook or notepad, whatever works for you. The important part is that you take stock of each week's effort and check in with how it made you feel. Once you've got week one under your belt, you can choose a different focus area for the following week.

TIP

Use the Buddy System

Call on your Aging Mastery® team for encouragement as you start a new activity and work toward your personal goal. Report your progress to them on a regular basis (via phone, e-mail, an app, etc.). Better yet, enlist them to do an activity with you. That way, you'll make one another accountable to achieve your goals.

A Sample AMP Day

The goal of AMP is to get you doing **positive activities that fit into your daily life**. We're convinced that once you start paying attention to your life in a holistic way, you'll be incorporating the Aging Mastery® Guideposts into your life naturally. They will become second nature! The illustration below shows how this would work:

Sample AMP Day

In this illustration, our AMP role model wakes up and has a good breakfast (*Health and Well-Being*) while attending to her budget (*Finances and Future Planning*). At mid-morning, she goes for a 30-minute walk (*Health and Well-Being*) all the while singing to the music she's listening to (*Creativity and Learning*). In the afternoon, she meets a friend (*Connections and Community*) and shares a story about her life (*Legacy and Purpose*). In the evening, she reflects on three things she's grateful for and meditates for 10 minutes (*Gratitude and Mindfulness*). Without too much effort, she has incorporated all six dimensions of aging into one day!

We hope that this illustration encourages you to think about the many ways that you are already "aging masterfully" and gives you ideas for how to structure your days to incorporate all six dimensions of aging well.

AMPlify Your Behavior

Many of us underestimate our efforts. Make sure you're acknowledging all of the hard work you're putting into reaching your Aging Mastery® Guideposts. For a week or two, write down everything you do from the minute you get up until bedtime. Look at what you are already doing and see how these activities align with the Aging Mastery® Guideposts.

Do's ✓	Don'ts ✗
Focus on changing behavior in one dimension of aging at a time to start.	Tackle all six dimensions right away.
Set small, manageable goals.	Set unattainable or complex goals.
Track your progress. Try different ways of tracking your journey (notebook, calendar, etc.) to find what helps you most in setting goals, recording progress, and reaching milestones.	Passively participate. Passive participation might cause you to ignore or lose track of your progress, or to minimize your milestones and achievements.
Incorporate activities into your down time. If you are waiting for an appointment, for example, use the time to write a thank-you note to a friend.	Assume you don't have enough time. To prove this, keep a daily time diary to see how you spend your time every day.
Create accountability. Recruit friends and family to do activities with you.	Make excuses that are easy to accept.
Be kind to yourself. If you miss a day or a week exercising, don't worry—just start up again and reset tomorrow.	Punish yourself if you get off track. Tomorrow is a new day!
Celebrate small wins. Give yourself credit for daily and weekly milestones. Reward yourself with something that motivates you. Sometimes progress is the best reward; sometimes, it's cake!	Lose sight of your progress.

3.2 ACTIVITIES FOR EACH DIMENSION OF AGING WELL

It's time to put what you've learned into practice. We've included a variety of activities. Some are "bite-sized" activities that you could (and should) do on a daily basis. These are things that you should strive to turn into regular habits! Other activities—such as creating a budget or going on a field trip with a friend—are things you'd do once a month or once a year.

In order to help you organize your time, we've noted about how long each activity should take. Anything 30 minutes or less can be considered a daily activity, while 60+ minute activities are things you'll do once a week, a month, or a season.

One final note: Consider these activities as springboards to help you change behaviors and achieve all Aging Mastery® Guideposts that make sense for you. Most importantly, feel free to adapt and tailor the activities to your needs and abilities.

TIP
Reward Yourself!

Seeing progress is an important part of motivation as we move toward a goal. One option for tracking progress is to create a "tip" jar for a particular goal. Each time that you take an action toward that goal, "tip" yourself. As the jar fills, you'll have tangible proof of progress toward the goal. When the jar is full, spend the money on something meaningful or recycle the money on "tips" toward your next goal!

♡ Gratitude and Mindfulness		
Activity	**What to Do**	**Estimated Time**
Daily Thanks	Start or end the day by writing down three things that you're grateful for. You can note these things in a journal, on a notepad, or on a sticky note.	5 min
Meditation Building Blocks	Create the foundation for a meditation practice. Reserve a quiet space in your home and pick a time for your daily meditation.	10 min
Bright Spot	Write down an event from the day or week that made you feel good. Note why it made you feel that way. Was it something out of the ordinary?	5 min
Moving Meditation	Go for a walk. Concentrate on moving slowly and smoothly, paying attention to the small and large movements your body is making. Breathe deeply and clear your mind as much as possible.	20 min

♥ Gratitude and Mindfulness		
Activity	**What to Do**	**Estimated Time**
Inspirational Focal Point	Print out a quote that inspires you and hang it somewhere you'll see it daily (like your fridge, bathroom mirror, in your wallet, or on the cover of your journal). If you need ideas, take a look at the AMP Facebook page (facebook.com/AMP).	10 min
Memory Workout	Practice Active Attention as described at the end of the Gratitude and Mindfulness section (2.1) of this book.	10 min
Routine Adjustment	Habits can be good but can also prevent us from exploring our world to the fullest. Try changing up one element of your daily routine today to get a fresh perspective on things. For example, instead of automatically watching the morning news, call a friend and make plans for an outing.	10 min

	Health and Well-Being	
Activity	**What to Do**	**Estimated Time**
Fitness Game Plan	Think about the obstacles that are between you and a regular fitness routine. Write down all the excuses you have for skipping exercise on a given day. For each excuse, list a workaround. Example: "I don't go to the gym because it's too crowded, BUT I could walk around the neighborhood or do yoga at home."	20 min
Rainbow Menu	Aim to get a mix of colors on your plate at every meal. Try for four cups of raw or two cups cooked vegetables a day, plus two servings of fresh fruit. If that sounds intimidating, ask friends or family members for recipe suggestions or look online.	10 min

Health and Well-Being		
Activity	**What to Do**	**Estimated Time**
Self-Care Check-In	Answer this question: Did I do something to improve my health today? Reflect on what you did (or didn't do), how it made you feel, and what you can do tomorrow to improve your health.	10 min
Drink Up!	Work with your medical team to understand your hydration needs, keeping in mind that the average is 64 oz., then aim to drink that much water every day. If you have trouble drinking plain water, try adding lemon or cucumber slices.	5 min

	Health and Well-Being	
Activity	**What to Do**	**Estimated Time**
Medical Appointment Prep	Feel more confident and get the most out of your next doctor's visit by doing the following: • List everything you want to discuss and prioritize your concerns. • Describe your symptoms. • Note any health or life changes. • Bring medication list, insurance cards, and medical records (if needed). • Have a friend/family member join you (optional).	15 min

![piggy bank icon] Finances and Future Planning		
Activity	**What to Do**	**Estimated Time**
Penny Saved, Penny Earned	Do you ever spend money on something and regret it later? Be mindful of your spending. Think of one way you can change your normal spending pattern to use money wisely and have more money in the bank.	10 min
Budget Builder	Clear your schedule, gather your paperwork, and get comfortable. Now, create or review your weekly, monthly, and yearly budgets. Online tools such as EconomicCheckUp® (EconomicCheckUp.org) can help as can many software programs.	60 min

Finances and Future Planning		
Activity	**What to Do**	**Estimated Time**
Home Reality Check	Assess your housing situation every few months and keep alternative living arrangements in mind: • Is my home the right size for me? Can I move about it easily and maintain it? • Do I feel safe at home and in my community? • Are there people nearby whom I can ask for help? • Can I safely get to where I need to go? • Do I have money for major repairs and can I afford the costs of my home (mortgage, insurance, etc.)?	30 min

Finances and Future Planning		
Activity	**What to Do**	**Estimated Time**
Your Future Self	Write down two things that brought you joy today that you want to continue to be able to do in the future. (Example: I want to keep up my singing lessons and live close to my friends.) What financial and housing decisions do you need to make now to ensure you can still do those things?	10 min
Finance Clean-up	Do one task today to tidy up your finances: 1. Set up online bill payment/banking. 2. Cut up credit cards that you don't use or that have high interest rates. 3. Shred old financial documents and account statements. 4. Assess and/or appraise valuables and collectibles. Aim to make it through the entire list every few months.	10–60 min

Connections and Community		
Activity	**What to Do**	**Estimated Time**
Reconnecting	Reach out to a friend or family member whom you haven't connected with in some time. You'll be surprised at how easy it is, and how good it makes you feel—not to mention them!	10 min
Social Ventures	• Volunteer in your community • Take a class that interests you • Join a group or club • Plan a trip with an organization • Attend community events If mobility or transportation issues prevent you from doing these activities in person, look for ways to interact virtually such as making phone calls for a help line or joining an online book club.	60 min or more

Connections and Community		
Activity	**What to Do**	**Estimated Time**
Handling Touchy Situations	Review (and memorize) these tips and apply them the next time you are in a difficult situation: • Make eye contact • Listen before speaking • Think carefully about what you want to say and how you want to say it • Let the other person know it's OK to disagree • Don't hold your breath (as it creates tension in you and others)	10 min
Circle of Support	On a sheet of paper, draw several circles. Within each circle, list one person—a friend, family member, colleague, trusted professional, etc.—and describe how they support you. Are there areas in which you could use more support? Who are others who could help you? How can you help those in your circle?	20 min

Creativity and Learning		
Activity	**What to Do**	**Estimated Time**
Artful Relaxation	Drawing and coloring are great activities for focusing your mind and decompressing—in addition to helping you release your creative juices. Draw or doodle something freehand, or pick up a coloring book. Color outside the lines for a change of pace!	15 min
Mind Expedition	Begin to explore a new topic today. Pick up a book, watch a documentary, or listen to a podcast on a topic you've always wanted to learn about. Podcasts and audiobooks are great for learning on the go.	20 min
Improv Act	Make something from whatever is available to you or do something new without preparation. For example, make a healthy snack or dessert from whatever ingredients you have on hand. Or, go to a gym and take a new exercise or dance class.	10–20 min

	Creativity and Learning	
Activity	**What to Do**	**Estimated Time**
Playtime!	Do something unexpected. Put on that silly hat and go for a walk, or tell someone a new joke.	10 min
Field Trip	Head out on a field trip to a local park, museum, historic house, or other favorite place. Invite a friend or family member along. If mobility or transportation issues prevent you from doing these activities, take an online field trip. Many museums, for example, showcase their collections online.	60 min or more
Listen Up!	Listen to one of your favorite songs. Then, search in your own music collection or online (or at your local library) for another version of the same song. What is different about the two versions? What do you like about each one? How would you sing the song if you were on stage?	10–20 min

	Legacy and Purpose	
Activity	**What to Do**	**Estimated Time**
Memory Lane	Share a memory with a family member or friend and ask them to do the same. It's great to share details about your past, your family history, or moments that were important to you.	10 min
Back to the Future	Are there any activities or trips you'd like to do again? Make a list of things that you enjoyed doing in your past and would like to do again. Then, come up with a plan to make them happen!	30 min
Skills Dividend	You've acquired many incredible skills. Maybe it's making pie crusts. Maybe it's knowing how to fix a car or play an instrument. Whatever your strengths, pay these out in dividends to others and share your wealth of knowledge with the world.	60 min or more

✿ Legacy and Purpose

Activity	What to Do	Estimated Time
Heritage Food	Recipes preserve family history. Write down the recipes for 2-3 dishes that you love cooking—and that you're known for. Share these with friends and family members. Better yet, invite them over to cook them with you!	60 min or more
Purpose Prize	Think of your life's purpose in terms of an award. Which award would you give yourself? (Examples: Best Problem Solver, Most Compassionate, Greatest at Making Others Smile.) Do this thought experiment from time to time to help you be mindful about connecting what you see as your purpose—or purposes!—to your actions.	10 min

	Legacy and Purpose	
Activity	**What to Do**	**Estimated Time**
"Senior" Achievement	Create a list of things you've accomplished. Include everything that's been meaningful to you, no matter how small it may appear to others. What makes the items on your list special? What other things do you still want to accomplish?	20 min

3.3 AGING MASTERY® GUIDEPOSTS

Gratitude and Mindfulness

	How often?	✓
I write down three things that I am grateful for.	Daily	
I meditate for 10 minutes.	Daily	
I notice and appreciate something small and wonderful.	Daily	
I am accountable and responsible for my actions.	Daily	
I set goals for each day.	Daily	
I reflect on my progress toward my goals.	Daily	
I express gratitude to people who make a difference in my life.	Weekly	
I focus on changing unwanted habits.	Weekly	

Health and Well-Being

I exercise for 30 minutes: a mix of aerobics, balance, strengthening, and flexibility.	4–5 days/week	
I eat a variety of foods that are nutrient-rich.	Daily	
I drink plenty of water and clear liquids.	Daily	
I use sleep strategies to maintain consistent sleep.	Daily	
I take medications and supplements as directed.	Daily	
I keep my home free from hazards that could cause a fall or injury.	Daily	
I practice proactive preventive health care.	Daily	
I encourage and support others to help them achieve their health and well-being goals.	Weekly	

Finances and Future Planning

I have a spending budget and keep to it.	Daily	
I am on the alert for financial scams.	Daily	
I do what I can to increase my income or reduce my expenses.	Weekly	
I keep important financial and personal records in order.	Monthly	
I review my Medicare and other insurance plans for both coverage and costs.	Yearly	
I assess my living situation and consider rightsizing options.	Yearly	
I have an advance care plan and keep it updated, and talk to my family about my end-of-life choices.	Yearly	
I meet with a financial planner and benefits advisor to review both my current and long-term needs.	Yearly	

Connections and Community

I practice small acts of kindness.	3–4 days/week	
I practice the art of communicating: listen, learn, lean in, and love.	Daily	
I have meaningful connections with people of other generations.	Weekly	
If I am a caregiver, I help myself. If not, I help a caregiver.	Weekly	
I spend time with friends and family.	Weekly	
I participate in a group (or groups) that align with my interests.	Monthly	
I am involved in civic causes and community projects to leave a legacy of positive change.	Monthly	
I repair or renew relationships that are neglected or frayed.	Monthly	

Creativity and Learning

I bring music into my life.	Daily	
I incorporate a sense of play into my life.	Daily	
I learn about a new topic or refresh my learning.	Weekly	
I start up—and keep up—a hobby.	Weekly	
I experiment and change the typical way I do things.	Weekly	
I question assumptions to spark new ways of thinking.	Weekly	
I create (arts, crafts, gardens, food, etc.)	Monthly	
I take part in cultural events.	Monthly	

Legacy and Purpose

I create pathways for my life's purpose to flourish.	Daily	
I apologize when I am in the wrong.	Daily	
I share my life story with others.	Daily	
I spend time each day in service to others.	Daily	
I share my knowledge with others.	Weekly	
I have created and act on a purposeful bucket list.	Monthly	
I participate in intergenerational activities.	Monthly	
I reflect on my responsibilities and my life's purpose.	Monthly	

ENDNOTES

1. Poem 1058, *The Complete Poems of Emily Dickinson*.

2. Social Security Administration, "Cohort Life Expectancy Table and CDC State-Specific Healthy Life Expectancy at Age 65 Years." www.ssa.gov/oact/tr/2012/lr5a4.html

3. Christensen, Kaare, et al. "Ageing populations: the challenges ahead." Lancet, October 2009. www.thelancet.com/journals/lancet/article/PIIS0140-6736(09)61460-4/abstract

4. U.S. Bureau of Labor Statistics, "American Time Use Survey," 2013

5. Rubin, Gretchen. *Better than Before: Mastering the Habits of Everyday Lives*. 2005.

6. Pink, Daniel H. *Drive: The Surprising Truth About What Motivates Us*. 2009.

7. "Tiny Habits w/ Dr. BJ Fogg - Behavior Change." www.tinyhabits.com

8. Emmons RA, et al. "Counting Blessings Versus Burdens: An Experimental Investigation of Gratitude and Subjective Well-Being in Daily Life." Journal of Personality and Social Psychology (Feb. 2003): Vol. 84, No. 2, pp. 377–89.

9. Grant AM, et al. "A Little Thanks Goes a Long Way: Explaining Why Gratitude Expressions Motivate Prosocial Behavior." Journal of Personality and Social Psychology (June 2010): Vol. 98, No. 6, pp. 946–55.

10. Sansone RA, et al. "Gratitude and Well Being: The Benefits of Appreciation," Psychiatry (Nov. 2010): Vol. 7, No. 11, pp. 18–22.

11. Huffman, et al. "Effects of Optimism and Gratitude After ACS." Circulation: Cardiovascular Quality and Outcomes (December 2015): www.ncbi.nlm.nih.gov/pmc/articles/PMC4720551

12. Keng, Shian-Ling. "Effects of Mindfulness on Psychological Health: A Review of Empirical Studies." Clinical Psychology Review (Aug. 2011): Vol. 31, No. 6, pp. 1041–1056. www.ncbi.nlm.nih.gov/pmc/articles/PMC3679190

13. Hayes AM, Feldman G. "Clarifying the construct of mindfulness in the context of emotion regulation and the process of change in therapy." Clinical Psychology: Science and Practice (2004): No. 11, pp. 255–262.

14. Kabat-Zinn, J. "Mindfulness-based interventions in context: Past, present, and future." Clinical Psychology: Science and Practice (2003): No. 10, 144–156. www.ncbi.nlm.nih.gov/pmc/articles/PMC3679190/#R83

15. National Center for Complementary and Integrative Health, National Institutes of Health, Department of Health and Human Services. "Mindfulness-Based Stress Reduction (MBSR) Information": www.nccih.nih.gov/taxonomy/term/228

16. Derived from NCCIH, NIH, HHS. "Meditation—In Depth": www.nccih.nih.gov/health/meditation/overview.htm

17. Everyday Memory is a program created by Robin West, Ph.D. www.everydaymemoryclinic.org/home.html

18. Adapted from National Council on Aging. "6 Ways to Eat Well as You Get Older": www.ncoa.org/resources/6-ways-to-eat-well-as-you-get-older-infographic

19. NIH, HHS. "Healthy Eating": www.nia.nih.gov/health/healthy-eating

20. World Health Organization. "Global Recommendations on Physical Activity for Health": www.who.int/dietphysicalactivity/physical-activity-recommendations-65years.pdf?ua=1

21. National Institute on Aging, HHS. "Go4Life": www.go4life.nia.nih.gov

22. Adapted from NCOA, "Take Control of Your Health: 6 Steps to Prevent a Fall": www.ncoa.org/healthy-aging/falls-prevention/preventing-falls-tips-for-older-adults-and-caregivers/take-control-of-your-health-6-steps-to-prevent-a-fall/

23. Adapted from NCOA, "Debunking the Myths of Older Adults and Falls": www.ncoa.org/healthy-aging/falls-prevention/preventing-falls-tips-for-older-adults-and-caregivers/debunking-the-myths-of-older-adult-falls

24. Adapted from Centers for Disease Control and Prevention, "Check for Safety: A Home Falls Prevention Checklist for Older Adults": www.cdc.gov/steadi/pdf/check_for_safety_brochure-a.pdf

25. Smith, Melinda et al. Helpguide.org, "Sleep Tips for Older Adults": www.helpguide.org/articles/sleep/how-to-sleep-well-as-you-age.htm

26. Helpguide.org, "The Biology of Sleep": www.helpguide.org/harvard/biology-of-sleep-circadian-rhythms-sleep-stages.htm

27. Smith et al.

28. Government Accountability Office. "Retirement Security: Most Households Approaching Retirement Have Low Savings." May– June 2015: www.gao.gov/products/GAO-15-419

29. Employee Benefit Research Institute. "The 2017 Retirement Confidence Survey: Many Workers Lack Retirement Confidence and Feel Stressed About Retirement Preparations": www.ebri.org/surveys/rcs/2017

30. Fidelity Viewpoints. "Retiree health care costs continue to surge," 6 Sept. 2017: www.fidelity.com/viewpoints/retirement/retiree-health-costs-rise

31. Shankar, Aparna and Anne McMunn et al. "Loneliness, Social Isolation, and Behavioral and Biological Health Indicators in Older Adults." Health Psychology (2011), Vol. 30, No. 4, pp. 377–385: www.pdfs.semanticscholar.org/ c468/3c7b9c807385fe85a2b341a20fd225d4ab4d.pdf

32. Cacioppo, John T. and Louise C. Hawkley "Perceived social isolation and cognition." Trends in Cognitive Sciences (Oct. 2009), Vol. 13, No. 10, pp. 447–454: www.doi.org/10.1016/j.tics.2009.06.005

33. Holt-Lunstad, Julianne et al. "Loneliness and Social Isolation as Risk Factors for Mortality." Perspectives on Psychological Science (March 2015), Vol. 10, No. 2, pp. 227–237: www.journals. sagepub.com/doi/abs/10.1177/1745691614568352

34. Elwert, Felix and Nicholas A. Christakis. "The Effect of Widowhood on Mortality by the Causes of Death of Both Spouses." American Journal of Public Health (November 2008), Vol. 98, No. 11, pp. 2092–2098: www.ncbi.nlm.nih.gov/pmc/articles/PMC2636447

35. Bookwala, Jamila; Kirsten I. Marshall; Suzanne W. Manning. "Who Needs a Friend? Marital Status Transitions and Physical Health Outcomes in Later Life." Health Psychology (2014), Vol. 33, No. 6, 505–515: www.apa.org/pubs/journals/releases/hea-0000049.pdf

36. Katsushika Hokusai: The Complete Works. "Biography of Katsushika Hokusai": www.katsushikahokusai.org/biography.html

37. Antczak, Stephen L. "Who Says Scientists Peak By Age 50?"

NextAvenue (5 Aug. 2014):
www.nextavenue.org/who-says-scientists-peak-age-50

38. Knowles, Malcolm. *Andragogy in Action*. San Francisco: Jossey-Bass, 1984.

39. Knowles, Malcolm. *The Adult Learner: A Neglected Species (3rd Edition)*. Houston: Gulf Publishing, 1984.

40. Cutts, Matt. "Try something new for 30 days." TedEd: www.ed.ted.com/lessons/try-something-new-for-30-days-matt-cutts

41. Duckworth, Angela. *Grit: The Power of Passion and Perseverance*. Scribner, 2016.

42. Ericsson, Anders and Robert Pool. *Peak: Secrets from the New Science of Expertise*. Eamon Dolan/Houghton Mifflin Harcourt, 2017.

43. Read the entirety of "Crossing Brooklyn Ferry" by Walt Whitman on the Poetry Foundation's website: www.poetryfoundation.org/poems-and-poets/poems/detail/45470

About the National Council on Aging

National Council on Aging

The **Aging Mastery Program**® is built on the collective wisdom of the National Council on Aging (NCOA) and its President & CEO Jim Firman. Both have devoted decades to improving the lives of older adults.

Founded in 1950, NCOA is the country's oldest national nonprofit focused on meeting the needs of older adults. Our vision is a just and caring society in which each of us, as we age, lives with dignity, purpose, and security.

NCOA is a national advocate for older adults. We laid the groundwork for critical programs like Meals on Wheels and successfully pushed for the laws that created Medicare, Medicaid, the Older Americans Act, and the Affordable Care Act.

For more than 65 years, NCOA also has worked with local organizations to help older adults find and apply for benefits programs, take classes to prevent falls, get training for a new job, and stay active and engaged in their communities. Many of our programs are delivered through local community groups, and others are available online.

Our experience has given us a deep understanding of the issues older adults face—and what really works to make their lives better. Under Jim Firman's leadership, we have assembled this knowledge into the **Aging Mastery Program**®.

On your **Aging Mastery**® journey, we encourage you to explore NCOA's other programs and services:

- **BenefitsCheckUp®** is a confidential website where you can discover if you're eligible for 2,000+ public and private benefits programs to help pay for medicine, rent, heat, and other daily costs. Enter some basic information, and you will get a personalized report, along with steps to apply.
- **EconomicCheckUp®** can help you make the most of your money, especially if you live on a fixed income. It includes online tools to make a budget, reduce debt, and get connected to training and jobs.
- **My Medicare Matters®** offers information and tools to help you choose the best Medicare plan for your situation—and make the most of your coverage.
- **The Falls Free® Initiative** is a national effort to reduce the number of falls and fall-related injuries among older adults. On NCOA's website, you can find simple tips to prevent a fall.
- **The National Institute of Senior Centers** helps local senior centers be the best they can—offering fun and educational programs for older adults in their communities.

NCOA is very proud to bring you the **Aging Mastery Program®**, and we wish you the best on your path ahead!

ACKNOWLEDGEMENTS

Shimon Peres, one of the founders of modern Israel, wrote: "You are as great as the cause you serve, and as young as your dreams."

For me, Aging Mastery® is a dream come true that reflects both NCOA's great cause and the beauty and potential of what we can dream and accomplish with our gift of longer lives.

I am grateful to Susan Stiles, my amazing co-collaborator, for working with me to curate the best of NCOA's collective wisdom about the science and art of aging well, and for writing most of this beautiful book.

I am grateful to the older people who shaped my life. My parents, Liuba and Jay Firman, who nurtured me and gave me love, courage, and the opportunity to pursue my dreams. To Arthur Flemming, Esther Peterson, Charles Fahey, Robert Butler, and many others who were mentors and friends. And to my wonderful colleagues, past and present, at NCOA and in the field of aging. It has been a privilege and great fun to collaborate with them to improve the lives of millions.

Thank you to Peggy, Gina, Redwoods, Jeremiah, Jamie, Edgar, and Julietta who love me, put up with me, and remind me what really matters. I am so proud of all of you. I am incredibly lucky to have such a wonderful family and friends.

Aging Mastery® started as a pilot program at five sites, and without them, it would not have succeeded. Thank you to Lynn Fields Harris and Meghan McCoy (Philadelphia, PA), Joanne Moore and Angela Sinnott (Duxbury, MA), Dianne Stone (Newington, CT), Bob Pitman (Columbus, IN), and Elizabeth Bernat (Charleston, SC) for launching this program with NCOA. Our community partners and funders—past, present, and future—are helping us grow AMP across the country.

What's next for me? I am grateful for this gift of time, and I hope to spend it wisely in service to a great cause and in pursuit of beautiful dreams.

Jim Firman

ACKNOWLEDGEMENTS

Speaking of gratitude . . . Jim and I have many people to thank for their roles in making this book a reality, especially: Matthew Baek for his illustrations that helped highlight several Aging Mastery® guiding principles; Ginnefine Jalloh for her patience and her brilliant book design work; Jean Van Ryzin for her insights and (most importantly) her editor's eyes; Vanessa Sink for her "I'll drop everything and help" attitude; Mollie Chen and Heather Dupré for their guidance and honest feedback; Hayoung Kye and Emily McDonald for their work in growing the Aging Mastery Program® nationwide; and, finally, Jacquelyn Hannan for her many, many talents and her considerable contributions to this book.

Jim's career mission has been to improve the lives of older adults everywhere. Mine has been to design information to spark thinking and to inspire people. This book is the result of those two elements coming together.

With gratitude,

Susan Stiles